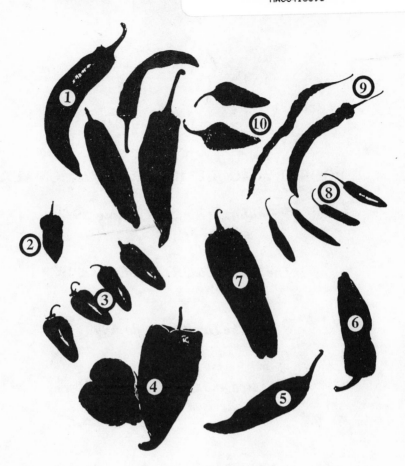

1. ANAHEIMS (GREEN AND RED)
2. FRESNO
3. JALAPEÑOS (GREEN TO RED)
4. POBLANOS
5. NEW MEXICO (SANDIA)

6. NEW MEXICO (BARKER)
7. NEW MEXICO (BIG JIM)
8. SERRANOS (GREEN TO RED)
9. CHILACA (PASILLA NEGRO)
10. GUEROS

BOOKS BY JACQUELINE HIGUERA MCMAHAN

California Rancho Cooking, **1983**

The Salsa Book, Revised Edition, **1989**

The Healthy Fiesta, **1990**

The Red and Green Chile Cookbook,
Revised Edition, **1992**

All books printed on recycled paper

RED AND GREEN CHILE COOKBOOK

Jacqueline Higuera McMahan

Photography, Robert McMahan

THE  OLIVE PRESS

RED AND GREEN CHILE COOKBOOK

THE OLIVE PRESS, MARCH 1992

LIBRARY OF CONGRESS CATALOG NUMBER

No. 87-091978

ISBN: 0-9612150-5-4

Printed in the United Sates of America
Revised Edition

To Ian and O'Reilly,

Who have grown up with chiles

Soy como el chile verde, Llorona,

picante pero sabroso.

CONTENTS

Photographs of Chiles

INTRODUCTION

One of my most haunting disappointments has
been the gradual disappearance of the simple-
cooking that was the crux of my mother's,
grandmother's, and aunts's kitchens. They
could make a pot of beans, some rice, and
tortillas into a feast. Just as many of the native
cooks do in the Southwest, the old California
cooks laid great claim to their Spanish ances-
tors usually omitting the debt they owed to
Mexico and the indigenous Indians from whom
they had borrowed many culinary ideas.

Chiles were the most persistent *tour de force* of the native kitchens and the key to authentic California and Southwestern cooking.

GOING BEYOND THE ETHNIC KITCHEN

When I was growing up with chiles, I didn't know we had an ethnic kitchen. It was a shock to discover that the food I loved like chorizo and red enchiladas were considered exotic. A college friend had to be resuscitated with bread and ice tea after the first bite of Grandma's mild tamales (for us, they were mild) and I thought it strange that someone could be that incapable of eating one of the four basic food groups.

Palates are changing and chiles are no longer a secret known only to native cooks. Up until now, the more unusual chiles could just be found in markets that served nearby Latin customers or you had to grow them or plead with your vegetable man to order them. Chiles are now IN and are more available than they ever were so progress has been made beyond the fifteenth century when a suspicious priest called Father Josè Acosta counseled that the use of chiles should be limited because they provoked lust. Chiles enjoyed their first rebirth when the Spanish explorers carried them back to Europe, erroneously thinking they were like the coveted spice, black pepper.

A second rebirth is occurring as cooking trends and thrill-seeking palates draw capsicums out of the ethnic and native kitchens. A new age is dawning and Father Acosta may have been right that chiles do provoke to lust. There is nothing like the passion of fresh con-verts. These lustful eaters have gone beyond the salsa that got them started.

THE MAGIC OF CHILES

At this very moment scientists are studying the X-quality that makes us eat chiles. Why do we want our mouths to burn? Is there too little excitment in otherwise predictable and ordered lives? Perhaps explaining the whys of chile's magic and its hold over us is like trying to apply logic to a searing love affair. We know one thing for sure. Chiles are unpredictable, capricious devils.

MYTHS ABOUT CHILES

There is a common notion held that the seeds are the hot part of a chile. Untrue. THE CHILE SEEDS THEMSELVES ARE NOT HOT, but when the oily capsaicin is released upon the seeds they taste hot. The clear, odorless, and flavorless globules of capsaicin are concentrated mainly along the placenta or veins. When the chile is picked or handled, these little globules break and spill their fire onto the wall of the chile and the seeds. The tip of any chile is always the mildest part because it is the furthest away from the main concentration of capsaicin globules. The top of the chile, closest to the stem, will always be the hottest part because it is closest to the glands where the capsaicin is produced.

Another notion currently being passed around is that chiles can make you high. We live in an age of highs: there are mountain highs, chocolate highs, sugar highs, and now even chile highs. I am still waiting. The wait is delicious but considering the amount of chiles I have consumed I must be hardened for the only levitation I have experienced is a full belly.

Many folk herbalists are convinced that a dose of chiles or "peppers" will take care of an ailing stomach. In the West Indies loss of appetite and mild indigestion are cured with mandram, an elixir made up of cucumbers, shallots, onions, lime juice, Madeira wine, and several pods of fiery bird pepper. Only be cautioned that the medicine will work if you have a good stomach but will kill you if you really need it!

RATING CHILES HEAT, A MYTH

There is no sure scientific way to rate the heat of chiles. The highly respected Scoville Organoleptic Test, invented in 1912, still relies on tasters who rate chiles with Scoville units, recorded in multiples of 100. It is difficult to measure the potency of something that has no taste, odor, or color. Tasters can never agree. What I consider to be a mild chile you might consider to be very hot. I decided not to complicate your lives with ratings and units because I do not agree with some of the Scoville ratings and you probably wouldn't either.

ANCIENT HISTORY

The chile dominates more aspects of cooking
styles and cuisines than any other single spice
or seasoning. From the studies of seeds found
in cave dwellings of Tehuacàn, Mexico, we
know that capsicum was being eaten as early as
7000 B.C. Now the chile is no longer ancient
history and it is being touted from Paris to
Tokyo.

CROSS-SECTION OF A CHILE POD

Stem ————————————————————

Capsaicin glands ———————————
(manufactures capsaicin) ————————

Placental crosswall
(Contains 89% of the heat) ——————

Veins (hot) ———————————————

Seeds ————————————————————

Placenta (hot) ——————————————

Skin (not hot) ——————————————

Chile flesh (not hot) ————————————

CHAPTER I

ANAHEIM GREEN CHILES

These are the mild chiles for people who cannot
stand the heat. Ninety percent of the time
Anaheims are as gentle as lambs particularly
when they are grown in damp climates such as
the Oxnard area of the California coast where
most of the green chiles canned by Ortega are
produced. A chile's personality is ultimately
determined by growing conditions. Anaheims

1

grown on the Mojave desert or in New Mexico are incendiary so one cannot assume that all Anaheims are mild.

Anaheims are found throughout the year in supermarkets but are the best during green chile season from July to October. During the late summer, you can usually find vegetable stands and small farmers selling their own crop of Anaheims. These home-grown chiles will often be smaller, more picante and more flavorful than the supermarket chiles which are likely to come from large commercial growers. Ripe, red Anaheims are available in the fall but should be used up quickly. Red chiles are at the last stage of ripening. The flesh of the red chile is sweeter just as the red bell pepper is sweeter than the green.

TO PREPARE GREEN CHILES FOR EATING AND COOKING

Anaheims, like all of the large chiles, need to have their tough, translucent skins removed before being used for salsa, rellenos, or stews. Figuratively speaking, large green chiles are wrapped in nature's cellophane. Much of their flavor lies under the skin so when you roast or

char them the flavor is greatly enhanced. Skin
them, it's not difficult.

There are several ways to skin a green chile.
You must blister and char the skin so you can
pull it off the chile. Most beginners do not
blacken the chile thoroughly enough. The
charring and blackening of the skin loosens it
for easier removal (and adds smoky flavor).
Listed below are the different methods:

METHOD 1: Impale the green chile on a long
fork (I use an old fondue fork) and hold over a
gas flame on your stove. Keep turning until the
chile is evenly blackened. I have become so
blasè about charring chiles that I usually have
four chiles at a time, each on its own Swedish
fondue fork, charring away, on my old Wolf
range. Two chiles take up each burner. When
completely blackened, place in a small paper
bag to steam for 5 minutes or let the chile cool
on the counter if you want a more crisp, un-
steamed texture. Peel off the blackened skin
and rinse in cold water. Slit each chile open on
one side and pull out the seeds. Rinse away
most of seeds.

IF YOU ARE SENSITIVE TO CAPSAICIN OIL, WEAR THIN PLASTIC GLOVES. Chile oil is strong and penetrating so you must wash your hands THOROUGHLY with detergent and hot water if you do not wear gloves. Do not touch your eyes, nose, or ears after peeling, seeding, and chopping chiles.

METHOD 2: If you have an electric stove just place a stainless steel cooling rack directly on the burner and turn heat to high. Place a couple of chiles at a time over the burner. Keep turning chiles until evenly blackened and blistered. Steam and peel.

METHOD 3: Place chiles five inches under broiler. Keep turning chiles until blackened. Chiles cook more using this method because of the contained heat of the broiler-oven but this is no problem if you are using the chiles for salsa or a stew. It is difficult to use broiler-flamed chiles for rellenos, where the chiles must remain intact, because they usually fall apart more easily than chiles blackened over a gas flame.

4

METHOD 4: Blacken chiles using a portable propane torch. The chiles remain wonderfully crisp and bright green but the unpredictability of the torch discourages some people. This is a good system to use if you have a bumper crop of chiles to char or you want to provide entertainment for your dinner guests. I have even used my little blow torch to melt the cheese over nachos.

METHOD 5: Char chiles over a barbecue grill. This is fun to do while you are grilling and gives the chiles a wonderful smoky flavor. Keep turning the chiles until the skins are loosened and charred.

METHOD 6: Roast chiles in a heavy skillet, griddle, or comal as cooks do in Mexico. This method is used with small chiles to ready them for grinding into salsas. The chile softens quite a bit as it cooks and roasts on the comal.

METHOD 7: If you live in New Mexico, you can stop by roadside stands where green chiles are being sold from August to October and then have them blistered on the spot in the chile roasters. I talked to one young woman who was purchasing 140 pounds of roasted chiles to make it through the long winter. The New Mexicans either freeze or dry the roasted green chiles.

HOW TO SKIN A CHILE

BLISTER AND BLACKEN THE SKIN EVENLY
STEAM IN PLASTIC BAG FOR 10 MINUTES
PEEL OFF LOOSENED SKINS
SLIT OPEN CHILE AND REMOVE SEEDS
RINSE IN COLD WATER

SKILLET CHILAQUILES, CAFE STYLE

Near the Alameda Park in Mexico City, is the charming Hotel De Cortes, originally a two-century old monastery. When we breakfasted in the courtyard, sipping our strong cafe con leche, we usually lingered a couple of hours over a second and third cup and conversations I can never recall.

The hotel's cook made the best chilaquiles I have ever tasted. Each order was simmered on top of the stove and delivered to the table in a piping hot skillet with a hand-embroidered cloth wrapped around the handle so you wouldn't burn yourself as you plunged into the treat. This method of cooking chilaquiles is the one used across the Republic in cafes and res- taurants. I have discovered recently that I like the simmering bottom heat of the skillet better than the oven method which is used by home cooks.

1/2 cup light oil, like Wesson
8 stale tortillas, cut into eighths
1/2 cup chopped onion
4 Anaheim chiles, charred, peeled, seeded
1 cup green tomatillo sauce, homemade or
storebought
1 cup chicken broth
1 sprig epazote, optional
2 sprigs cilantro

1 or 2 jalapeño chiles, fresh or canned, cut into
  rings
1/2 cup Monterey Jack cheese, grated
3 tablespoons Parmesan or Romano, finely
  grated
Pickled onions or avocado slices for garnish

1. It is important that you use corn tortillas that are at least a couple of days old. Stale tortillas will absorb much less oil, making chilaquiles a perfect way to use leftovers. I usually cut the tortillas into wedges and let them air dry a couple of hours before frying. Heat the oil in a 12-inch skillet (I use cast-iron) until almost smoking. Fry the tortilla wedges until a deep golden color. Drain on paper towels and blot well. If you do not fry them until they are crisp, the chilaquiles will be tough. I have even tried baking the wedges instead of frying them but the results are not as good.

2. Using a deep skillet that you can bring to the table, saute the onion in two tablespoons of the oil. When the onion is soft, add the green sauce, the broth, the herbs, and the tortilla wedges. Push the wedges down into the sim-mering liquid. Sprinkle the minced green chiles on top.

3. Simmer for about 10 minutes so the liquid will be absorbed by the tortillas and will thicken. Do not cook away all of the liquid. Halfway through the simmering sprinkle on the cheeses. When the cheese is melted and a few tablespoons of broth remain in the bottom of the skillet, you are ready to take the pan off the heat. Garnish with slices of jalapeño chile, some cilantro, some pickled onion, or avocado slices. This dish serves four for breakfast and six as a side dish. It is at its best when eaten immediately and does not stand in a warming oven which is why the cafes cook your order and then bring it sizzling to your table.

FRENCH BREAD CRUMB CHILE RELLENOS

These are not traditional but they are one of my favorite ways of preparing rellenos because they can be baked for a crowd, using jelly roll pans. The result is always crusty, golden chiles that everyone eats three or four of so make plenty. These chiles also reheat beautifully and much better than those done in an egg batter.

8-10 long green chiles (Anaheim or
   New Mexican type)
4 cups stale French or Italian bread, torn into
   pieces
1/4 cup Parmesan cheese, grated
1/4 pound Longhorn or Jack cheese, cut into
   sticks
1/4 cup melted butter
2 eggs
1 tablespoon water
1/2 cup flour

1. Blister and char chiles using your favorite method. Remove skins and seeds, leaving entire chile intact. Set aside. If you are rushed you could "get by" with canned green chiles in this recipe.

2. Place bread pieces in a blender or food processor and process until fairly fine. Try to achieve a fluffy texture.

3. Beat eggs with the water, placing in a wide bowl large enough to accomodate the size of a chile. Place the flour on a piece of waxed paper. Mix the crumbs and Parmesan cheese and place on another piece of waxed paper. Grease a jelly roll pan.

10

4. Place a stick of cheese inside each chile, dust with flour, dip the chile in the egg wash, and then place on the pile of breadcrumbs. Press the breadcrumbs onto the top of the chile and wherever needed. Now place chiles on the jelly roll pan and continue until all chiles are crumbed. Drizzle melted butter over the chiles and bake at 375 for 20 minutes or until they are golden and the cheese melted. You can also saute these chiles in a mixture of three tablespoons butter and three tablespoons oil but the baking technique is much easier. You will love these.

TEXAS CHICKEN FRIED CHILES

You will have a hard time choosing between the French Bread Crumb Chiles and a pile of these but there probably isn't anything, except an old shoe, that isn't good when chicken-fried.

10 -12 long green chiles (Anaheim or New Mexico-type)
1/2 pound longhorn cheese, cut into 3-inch sticks

2 cups thick buttermilk
1 cup flour
1/4 teaspoon ground cumin
1 teaspoon salt
1 teaspoon fine black pepper
2 cups light frying oil (Wesson or grapeseed)

1. Blister and char chiles according to your favorite method. Peel and seed, leaving chile intact. Cut a slit down the side of each chile and insert a stick of cheese.

2. Roll the stuffed chiles in the flour which has been blended with cumin, salt, and pepper.

3. Dip each floured chile in the buttermilk, allowing excess to drip off, and then dip each chile AGAIN in the flour. This production will result in chiles with a thick coating.

4. Fry two chiles at a time in hot oil until golden, turning once. Drain on several layers of paper towels. These Texas-style chiles are better than wonderful at a barbecue and you will always need more than you fixed. They're even good for breakfast with a sizzled, easy-over egg and biscuits.

NAKED STUFFED CHILES
WITH CHICKEN SALAD

Many of our California and Southwestern foods have traditionally been prepared in a particular way and never questioned for years. One of the good things to come out of our current food consciousness (and obsession) has been the rule breaking of young chefs. For instance, they did not assume that chiles rellenos always had to be battered and fried. Even though their originality can sometimes take exotic twists and turns, I applaud their fresh approach. Forgive me, Grandmama. After you have charred, steamed, and peeled your chiles try marinating them in a vinaigrette and then stuffing them with chicken salad or minced vegetables.

CHILES AND MARINADE:

6 fresh long green chiles (Anaheims)
1/3 cup olive oil
2 tablespoons wine vinegar
1 clove garlic, crushed
Salt and pepper to taste

CHICKEN SALAD FILLING:

1 whole chicken breast
1 red-skinned, new potato, diced
1 carrot, diced
2 tablespoons minced onion
1/4 cup frozen baby peas, thawed
1 tablespoon parsley, minced
1 tablespoon cilantro, minced
  (optional but good)
1/2 cup mayonaise
2 tablespoons sour cream
3 teaspoons of above marinade used for chiles

1. Prepare your marinade so that it is waiting for the chiles. Blister and char your chiles according to your favorite method. After charring, allow the chiles for this recipe to steam at least 15 minutes in a plastic bag as they will not be receiving further cooking. Then skin them carefully and cut a slit down the side to remove the seeds, leaving the stem on. Place in the marinade for at least two hours.

2. Simmer the chicken breast in water or chicken broth to cover for twenty minutes. Let it set in the broth (off the heat) for another five minutes. Remove, cool, and cut into cubes.

3. Simmer the diced potato and carrot in one-inch of water for about ten minutes or until just tender. Do not overcook as the vegetables will become mushy.

4. In a one-quart mixing bowl, place all the ingredients of the filling: the chicken cubes, potatoes, carrots, onion, peas, parsley, cilantro, mayonaise, sour cream, and a little marinade. Taste for seasoning, adding more marinade, salt, or freshly ground pepper.

5. Drain the chiles from the marinade. Stuff each one with about 1/4 cup of chicken salad. Lay out on a platter covered with lettuce leaves. Garnish with dabs of sour cream or creme fraiche and a cherry tomato for color. I serve these with corn muffins for lunch, a picnic, or a first course.

NAKED CHILES STUFFED WITH BLACK BEANS DRENCHED IN CHIPOTLE CREAM

CHILES:

6 fresh long green chiles (Anaheim or New Mexico type)

BLACK BEAN FILLING:

1 pound black beans, rinsed
1/2 onion, chopped
2 cloves garlic, minced
1 sprig epazote (optional but traditional)
1 chipotle chile en adobo, from can
1 and 1/2 teaspoons salt, added last 10 minutes

CHIPOTLE CREAM:

1 cup sour cream
2-3 tablespoons milk
1 teaspoon of mashed chipotle chile en adobo or dried chipotle, powdered

1. Blister and char the green chiles according to your favorite method. Steam in plastic bag for fifteen minutes. Remove skins. Slit chiles down the sides and remove seeds. Leave stems intact. You can do this while the beans are cooking. Refrigerate the chiles until they are needed.

2. Rinse beans in colander and pick over for stones. Place in four-quart pot and cover with water. Bring to boil and simmer for three minutes. Allow beans to steep for at least two hours.

3. Add the onion, garlic, epazote, and chipotle chile to the bean pot. Simmer for about one and a half hours. Because of the presoaking method, these beans will cook faster. Taste for seasoning. Add salt.

4. While the beans are cooking, make the chipotle cream. Thin out the sour cream with the milk and stir in the chipotle. I prefer to use the dried chipotle (see Resources), pulverizing it in a mortar. The dried chile is not as overpowering as the chipotle en adobo.

5. When ready to serve place about one-fourth cup black beans drained of excess liquid, in each green chile. Arrange on a heat-proof platter and place in a preheated 350 degree oven for ten minutes just to warm. You may serve each chile in a pool of chipotle cream or pour some of the cream over the top. Sprinkle the cream with a little dusting of mild chile powder or sweet paprika for color. This is a good treat for vegetarians but meat-eaters have been known to eat many of these.

RANCHO SARSA

This is California's original salsa as it was made by the rancheros who fondly called it "sarsa". I play a little with this recipe, adding and subtracting olive oil, or wine vinegar, and my trusty jalapeño magic (see Chapter IV) but basically it remains the same and just one of the treasures that my grandmother left me. Sarsa is as much a salad as it is a fresh salsa We love sarsa sandwiches which are just hunks of sour-dough bread piled with the stuff. You can melt cheese on top but that is complicating matters too much.

4 ripe, red tomatoes
4 long green chiles (mild Anaheims)
1/2 white or red onion, minced
1 or 2 canned jalapeño chiles, minced
1/4 cup fresh cilantro, snipped
1 tablespoon vinegar
1 tablespoon olive oil
1 clove garlic, minced

1. Blister the tomatoes over a gas flame or dip for 30 seconds in boiling water. Rinse in cold water and slip off the skins. If ripe tomatoes are out of season, substitute canned Italian plum tomatoes, well-drained, and one supermarket tomato, diced with the skin on.

2. Blister and char the green chiles according to your favorite method. Steam for five minutes in a plastic bag. Remove skins, stems, and seeds.

3. Chop the tomatoes and the green chiles. Do not put in food processor or blender.

4. Combine the tomatoes, green chiles, onion, jalapeños, cilantro, garlic, vinegar, and olive oil. Add salt to your taste. Sarsa keeps well for a day but then loses its fresh quality. Simmer

any leftover sarsa for five minutes in a saucepan and then it will keep for several days to be
used for dipping or as a sauce for huevos rancheros.

THE TAPIA FAMILY'S VEGETABLE
STEW WITH CHILES

The Tapias are a Mexican family who have
grown vegetables in the Los Angeles basin for
four generations. As civilization keeps infring-
ing on their cornfields, they are forced to find
other areas to farm. Their vegetables are picked
when they are bursting with sweet ripeness and
when I was testing recipes for *The Salsa Book* I
made daily runs on their tomatoes and chiles.
Beautiful Adela, from the Encino branch of the
family, shared one of the family's favorite
stews.

1 pound hot Italian sausage
1 flat red onion, chopped
1 clove garlic, minced
4 Anaheim chiles, charred, seeded, chopped
2 jalapeño or Fresno chiles, seeded, minced

4 ears of corn, kernels cut off the cob
3 ripe tomatoes, cored, chopped
1 can tomato sauce (8 oz.)
4 or 5 medium zucchini or crookneck squash,
  sliced
1 teaspoon black pepper
1/4 pound Cheddar cheese, grated
1/4 pound Monterey Jack cheese, grated

1. Slice the sausage and fry over medium heat until browned. Drain off all but two table-spoons of the fat. Saute the onion and garlic for three minutes. Add the chiles, corn, tomatoes, sauce, and zucchini. Simmer for 45 minutes to one hour over medium heat with an occasional stir. Sprinkle the cheese over the top and simmer until melted. You can prepare the stew in the morning and reheat the stew later with the cheese, and bring to a covered dish supper, potluck, or barbecue. The Tapias serve it with warm flour tortillas.

THE TAPIA FAMILY'S CORN PUDDING
(OR CHEPPOS)

The Tapia aunts are famous for their cheppos (little green corn tamales) but they thought up this quick version baked in a cazuela lined with green corn husks when they did not want to take the time to make individual tamales.

12 ears fresh corn (not frozen)
2 tablespoons flour
1/4 cup butter, room temperature
1/2 teaspoon salt
1 teaspoon sugar
1 teaspoon baking powder
1 cup sour cream
5 Anaheim green chiles, charred, peeled,
  seeded, cut into strips

1. Cut off ends of corn. Unfurl husks so as to leave intact. Blanch the reserved husks in several inches of boiling water for 1 minute to make pliable. Drain on paper towels and use the softened husks to line a two-quart casserole dish or cazuela. This step adds greatly to the flavor of the corn pudding.

2. Stand ears of corn in a large bowl and cut off kernels. Place kernels in the work bowl of food processor and roughly puree, leaving some texture. Next add the flour, butter, salt, sugar, baking powder, and sour cream. Pulse to blend.

3. Pour half of this mixture into the lined cazuela. On top, place the strips of green chile and then pour the rest of the corn-sour cream mixture on top. Place more blanched corn husks on top of the pudding. Bake in a pre-heated 350 degree oven for one hour. Allow the pudding to rest for 10 minutes before serving.

DRIED RED CALIFORNIA CHILES

When Anaheim chiles turn red and are dried, they are called California chiles. They are considered mild in comparison to other chiles and they are only hotter than a sweet bell pepper. When September comes, most green chiles begin to ripen and turn red. Often green chiles that you have stored in your refrigerator will gradually turn red.   Red chiles should be picked in early autumn, before the frost, and sun-dried in order to retain their inherent sweetness.

Dried California chiles are a dark burnished red in contrast to their bright red look alike cousins from New Mexico. Likewise, California ground chile will have a deeper color than the brighter New Mexican chile powder.

HOMEMADE CHILE POWDER

Rinse dried chiles in cold water to get rid of the field dust and lay them on a baking sheet. Place in a warm 300 degree oven for five minutes to dry. Break open each chile and shake out the seeds and remove the yellowish veins. Remove the dried stems.   Pulverize the pieces of chile in an electric coffee grinder, reserved for spices and chiles only, or use a blender. Use this homeground chile powder for stews, chiles, or sauces.

I make up a seasoning powder using three parts ground chile, one part ground cumin seed, one part dried Greek oregano, one part dried thyme, one part garlic powder, and one part onion powder. If you purchase whole dried chiles or chile powder that seems bitter it can be due to two causes: the chiles were struck by a harsh frost or they were commercially dried too quickly in hot ovens instead of being sun-dried as they do in New Mexico. PROPERLY DRIED RED CHILES SHOULD HAVE A LINGERING SWEETNESS AND NOT A BITTER AFTERTASTE.

HOMEMADE CHILE SAUCE

This one red sauce, made from dried, red chiles is the essential key to authentic California and Southwestern cooking and will be your claim to greatness as a chile cook. If your chiles are good, your sauce will be good. Choose dried chiles that have an even red color, unblemished by yellowish or dark spots, which can indicate infestation or old age. If I do not use up my ristra chiles in three months, I remove the chiles from the strings and freeze them in plastic bags. After six months of hanging in the light, dried chiles can pale and become infested.

15 dried California chiles (you can use half
*   ancho or New Mexican chiles)*
Boiling water to cover
1 clove garlic
Water
3 tablespoons oil
2 tablespoons flour
Chile puree
1 teaspoon oregano
Pinch of salt, ground cumin, powdered cloves
2 tablespoons vinegar
1/2 cup to 2 cups chicken, turkey or beef broth
*   for thinning out sauce*

1. Remove the stems, seeds, and veins from the chiles. Rinse them off in cold water and place in a large bowl with the clove of garlic.

2. Pour boiling water over the chiles. Allow them to steep for at least one hour with a lid over the top of the bowl so they steam.

3. Place one-third of chiles at a time in a blender jar with one-half cup of fresh water and the clove of garlic. Puree. Puree the rest of the chiles, adding about one-half cup of fresh water to each batch.

4. Push this puree through a wire strainer into a bowl to remove the bits of skin.

5. Prepare your roux by heating the oil in a large skillet. Stir in the flour and cook until golden, not brown. Next add the chile puree, the spices, the vinegar, and enough broth to make a sauce consistency. The amount of broth you ultimately add will depend upon how much water you added to the chiles when you were pureeing.

6. Simmer the chile sauce for about 20 minutes to blend flavors. Taste to see if you would like to add more spices. Makes about one quart of Chile Sauce for enchiladas or stews.

CARNE CON CHILE

On the ranchos of Spanish California, carne con chile (known in other places as chile colorado) was as dear to the paisanos as chili is to Texans. The staple in our family kitchen was red chile puree and my first cooking duty was to stand on a wooden stool and push soaked chiles for this stew through a cone-shaped sieve.

3 and 1/2 pounds chuck roast or rump roast
1/4 cup olive oil
2 medium white onions
6 cloves garlic, minced or use press
1 tablespoon cumin seeds, toasted
1 tablespoon oregano, toasted
3 cups homemade chile puree (see recipe above)
2 and 1/2 cups beef stock
2 or 3 tablespoons masa harina
1/4 cup water
Chopped cilantro to taste
1 cup pitted black olives for garnish

1. Cut meat into two-inch cubes and dry well with paper towels. Brown cubes in batches in

two tablespoons oil at a time in a heavy skillet, preferably of cast-iron If meat is not crowded, it will brown better.

2. Set browned meat aside and saute the onions until they begin to carmelize, about 15 minutes. Next add the garlic and the broth, scraping the browned bits off the bottom of the pan as the pan. Add all of the meat cubes back to the pan. Simmer for one to one and a half hours or until meat is tender. Then drain off all but one cup of broth.

3. To make the chile puree, follow steps one through four of the preceding recipe for Home-made Chile Sauce.

4. Toast your cumin seeds in a skillet for two minutes until they give off a little puff of cumin essence but are not browned just toasted. During the last minute, add the oregano to the same skillet and toast. Set aside.

5. Stir the chile puree and toasted spices into the meat and simmer for one more hour.

6. Add salt to your taste. Blend the masa harina and water into a smooth paste and

quickly stir into the stew to thicken. Serve this chile in big rustic bowls, garnished with cilantro and black olives. Serve beans on the side

MAMA'S THICK BEANS

To complicate these beans, would be like complicating biscuits and all the other things that are exquisite in their simplicity. You should not tamper with something so basically good as beans, water, a bone, and salt and pepper. In Querètaro, Mexico, where we lived for three years, plump beans in a thin, watery broth, were traditionally served in soup bowls at the end of the meal, but I favor my mother's beans ,thick enough to wrap in a tortilla.

1 pound pinto or pink beans
Water to cover
l onion, chopped
2 cloves garlic, minced
l piece of ham bone or l ham hock
   (optional but good)
Salt and pepper to taste

1. Put beans in a sieve and rinse with cold water. Sort the beans, looking for pebbles and other artifacts.

2. Put beans in three or four-quart pot and cover with water. Bring to a boil and simmer for three minutes. Take off the heat and let the beans steep for two to four hours.

3. Pour off the soaking water completely. You will lose a minimum of nutrients but you will greatly improve the digestibility of the beans. Cover the beans with eight cups of fresh water. Add the onion, garlic, and ham bone.

4. Simmer the beans for two hours on low heat. Keep hot water in the tea kettle so you may add water when necessary to keep the beans completely covered with liquid. Water should be at least one-inch above beans. Push across the bottom of the pot now and then with a wooden spoon to make sure that nothing is sticking. When the beans are tender, you may add salt judiciously. Remember that the ham bone will impart salt.

5. Now here is the important part that will

make your beans thick and famous. If your bean pot has a great deal of liquid, drain some off and reserve. Heat the fat or oil in a frying pan, and sprinkle in one-half teaspoon fine pepper. Now add one-half cup beans and one cup reserved bean liquor and mash while the beans and liquid are simmering. Next add one-fourth cup whole beans and a little more bean liquid. Again, keep mashing until you have a thick gruel with a few beans. I use a huge wooden spoon from Mexico to keep stirring and pressing the bean puree as it simmers. I witnessed this ritual many times in our kitchen and somehow the process cannot be duplicated using a blender to puree the beans.

6. Stir the puree back into the big pot of beans and put on simmer. Now keep adding a little more reserved bean liquor at a time so the beans slowly thicken. You may end up using all of the reserved bean liquor. Remember, you must stir and press with your big spoon. This should not take more than 20 minutes of con-centration. Most of the beans remain whole but in a thick broth.

These beans were the ones served at our ranch

for barbecues and if we were invited to a party, my mother was always asked to bring her beans.

REFRIES

Mama's Thick Beans are already halfway there to becoming refries. Lard, bacon grease, or a good oil are necessary for refries since we like them almost like a bean pancake, crispy and sizzled around the edges. You really should use a well-seasoned cast-iron skillet for this operation.

2 or 3 cups cold beans, cooked the day before
4 tablespoons fat or oil
3 tablespoons dry Romano cheese , grated

1. Heat the fat in your skillet and then dump in the beans. Let them sizzle away for a few minutes and mash them while they are sizzling. Leave some texture and some beans whole. The whole process shouldn't take more than 15 minutes. Sprinkle the top with the grated cheese. These refries are perfect alongside huevos rancheros, on tostados, or nachos.

Bean note: Canned refried beans can actually be quite good if you sizzle and refry them in a heavy skillet and sprinkle with Parmesan or Jack cheese

TAME CHILI FOR GRINGOS AND LITTLE CHILDREN

In the enlightened age of chile appreciation, there still exist those who do not subscribe to the pleasure-pain principle and there are fewer gringos now than there ever was. They deserve sympathy and a good bowl of mild red.

2 tablespoons oil
1 onion, chopped,
2 pounds ground sirloin
3 cloves garlic, minced
2 tablespoons mild chile powder
  (California or ancho)
1 tablespoon cumin powder
1 tablespoon oregano

1 teaspoon cinnamon
1 teaspoon garlic salt
3 large cans of stewed tomatoes
1 large can premium kidney beans (1 lb.,ll oz.)
1/2 round of Ibarra sweet Mexican chocolate or
substitute 2 teaspoons bitter cocoa powder
Chicken broth or tomato juice for thinning chile
if necessary

1. Saute the onion in the oil until translucent.
Remove from skillet and set aside.

2. Using the same skillet, fry the meat until it is
somewhat browned.
Drain off any fat in the pan.

3. Add the garlic, chile powder, spices, and the
stewed tomatoes with their juice. It helps if
you break up the tomatoes with your hands or
roughly chop. Kids are suspicious of big pieces
of tomato (it might be good for them).   Simmer
for 45 minutes. Taste to see if you would like
to add more chile powder.

4. Add the chocolate, chopped into small
pieces, or the cocoa powder and the kidney

beans. If the chile is too thick, thin it out with broth or tomato juice. If you would like it thicker, mix two tablespoons masa harina with one-fourth cup water. Stir and blend into the chile and simmer 10 minutes more.

Chile note: if you are making mild chile, you can add color by using one or two tablespoons of sweet Hungarian paprika. Santa Cruz Chili Paste from Arizona is also a good substitute for chile powder and makes a wonderful mild chile. See Resources.

CHAPTER II

NEW MEXICAN CHILES

There is one thing we have to get straight immediately. There are many types of New Mexican chile and they are wildly different. A simple questioning of a native New Mexican's favorite chile is equivalent to quibbling with a New Orleans taxi driver over red beans and rice. You don't! Within New Mexico, where chiles reign supreme, chiles are not simply rated, as outsiders are wont to do, but they are discussed as seriously as wines from different regions.

THERE ARE DIFFERENT TYPES AND THERE IS GREAT FAVORITISM AS TO WHERE THOSE TYPES ARE GROWN. There are modern cultivars from Anaheim seed such as the Sandia, the Big Jim, and the very mild Number 6-4 grown by commercial growers which in fact has become so mild the natives are complaining. The word is out that some farmers are trying to put some heat back in the chile.

The pungent, hot Sandia has a lot more personality when compared to the thick, fleshy Numex Big Jim which was cultivated to appease the gringo palate. But I love the Big Jim for rellenos and I like the fact that it does not anesthetize my taste buds. Most New Mexicans prefer the Sandia or the even smaller, hotter Barker chile.

The true Indian Chimayo chile grown in the Chimayo area of northern New Mexico, is sought out by devoted aficionados for its flavor and hint of sweetness. There is a purity of taste in the more ancient strains of primitive chile, less touched by technology. The heat comes at the palate in delicious waves of pleasure-pain.

These local chiles, originating in northern New Mexico, are smaller and more thin-walled, making them difficult to peel when green so they are rarely available when fresh but their rich, ground powders, made from the dried, red chiles, are the best in the world.

Within New Mexico, there are regional loyalties between the northern and southern parts of the state and this determines whether you buy the chiles grown in Las Cruces, Hatch, or north to Espanola and San Juan Pueblo. And then there are variations around every little hill and vale. Any respectable New Mexican could tell you which mound of dirt produces the most flavorful chiles. For green chiles the magic word is Hatch. Chiles grown in this southern area of New Mexico are sought after in late August and September. During the brief period when green chiles are being harvested, the New Mexicans will purchase a bushel of roasted chiles to freeze or dry.

You can dry the roasted, peeled green chiles by hanging them covered with cheesecloth on a clothesline in the sun or dry slowly in a food dehydrator. Store dried chiles in plastic bags. Dried green chiles are given a good soak in hot water for several hours to reconstitute and then they can be used in soups and stews or salsas. They revive beautifully with the advantage of already being peeled and have a much better flavor than chiles which have been frozen. You can use them in any recipe except those requiring whole chiles such as for rellenos. If you have them on hand you need never suffer a day without green chile. See Resources for purchasing dried green chile.

In Latin families, the cazuela is a prized cooking vessel of terra cotta and from within its depths comes the food that nurtures body and spirit. When the cazuela in our family was emptied, it was quickly filled again with a soup or beans and returned to its proper positon on the back burner where it could simmer undisturbed.

Cazuela cooking embraces everything that makes a kitchen memorable with smells of garlic, onion, spices, chiles, olive oil, and a caring. Chile verde symbolizes this style of cooking and everyone in New Mexico knows that they have the best recipe. Below is my version, fashioned after my favorite chile verde as prepared by a transplanted New Mexican chef in Santa Barbara.

CHILE VERDE

This classic dish of the Southwest is abundant with fresh green chiles and is one of the hottest of the chile specialties. You can use either New Mexico green chiles (dried or fresh) or the Anaheims grown in California but it would be a sacrilege to use canned chiles. To be traditional, this stew should make beads of sweat break out on your brow, making it the perfect dish for cold weather.

1 tablespoon oregano, 2 teaspoons ground cumin,
  1 teaspoon sage,1/2 teaspoon pepper, 1/2 teaspoo.
  cayenne pepper
3 and 1/2 pounds pork roast or pork loin

2 medium onions, chopped
6-8 cloves garlic, minced
4 tablespoons oil
2 bay leaves
1 can beer, 12 ounces
1 quart chicken or turkey broth
10 green chiles, Anaheim or New Mexican type
2-8 jalapeños, stems and seeds removed,
    minced
1 bunch carrots, peeled, cut into 2-inch chunks
3 russet potatoes, cut into chunks
Cilantro, optional (used in Mexico but not in
    the Southwest)

1. Cut meat into two-inch pieces and rub thoroughly with the spice blend. Brown the meat in three batches, using two tablespoons of oil at a time and adding more when necessary.

2. When meat is all browned, set aside and saute the onion, adding the garlic at the end. Drain any excess oil from the pan.

3. Return meat to the pan with the onion and garlic. Pour in the beer. Simmer briskly and then add the broth and the bay leaves. Cook for 30 minutes.

4. Char the large chiles using your favorite method. Peel, seed, and stem. Chop the green chiles and the fresh jalapeños you wish to use and then stir all of the chiles into the simmering meat. Cook for 45 minutes and add the potatoes and carrots. Simmer until the vegetables are tender but not mushy, about 25 minutes. Salt to taste and adjust seasonings.

CHILE NOTE:

Always be brave concerning chile. After your first bite of green chile you will be hooked. The capsaicin oil found in all chiles activates the salivating process, your body's way of a cool down after a melt down. This miracle of nature actually then stimulates your taste buds and your taste buds will want more.

BURRITO GREEN CHILE

This is for my boys, who want it fast and simpler than the preceding version.   As far as fillings go, this is one of the most flavorful that you will find for burritos, tacos, and tostados. This recipe works very well with dried, green chiles.

1 and l/2 pounds green chile, Anaheim or New
  Mexico
1 and 1/2 cups water
1 chicken boullion cube
l/2 cup chopped onion
1 pound lean hamburger
2 cloves garlic, mashed through garlic press
1 teaspoon cumin powder
2 teaspoons flour
1 tablespoon water

1. Char the chiles over a gas flame or under a broiler until blackened and blistered. Remove skins, stems, and seeds. Mince with knife or in food processor. You can substitute canned or dried chiles for fresh.

2. Simmer chiles in water with boullion and chopped onion for 20 minutes. The liquid should reduce by one-half cup.

3. Meanwhile, brown the hamburger in a skillet, adding the pressed garlic and cumin.

4. Lift the hamburger into the simmering chiles. Stir in the flour which you have blended with water. Simmer for 20 minutes or until thickened.

NEW MEXICO GREEN CHILE SAUCE

In New Mexico, it is sometimes confusing when an outsider tries to distinguish between the Chile Verde that is a stew, the one that is a sauce, and the one that is a soup. Sometimes they are all pretty closely related depending upon the cook's whim. This recipe for green chile sauce is the one that you can pour over everything but dessert if you want to live like the natives. It is good over huevos rancheros, potatoes, enchiladas, and burritos, and knowing

the whimsicality of cooks, you'll find something to put it on that I haven't thought of yet.

10 fresh green chiles, Anaheim, Big Jim, or
   Sandia
1/2 cup onion, minced
2 cloves garlic, minced
2 tablespoons oil
1 can chicken broth
1 and 1/2 cups water
2 teaspoons flour
Pinch of ground cumin
1 teaspoon salt

1. Char, peel, seed, and stem the chiles according to the directions in Chapter I. Chop very
fine.

2. Saute the onions and garlic in oil until
golden. Place all the rest of the ingredients but
the flour and cumin in a large saucepan and
simmer for one-half hour. Make a paste with
the flour, cumin and two tablespoons water and
stir it into the green chile sauce to thicken just a
little. Simmer for 5 minutes. This is a superb
sauce to serve over the top of carne adovada
burritos.

CHILE NOTE For Green Chile Soup: exchange one quart of homemade or canned chicken broth for all of the liquid in the recipe. Combine with the required amount of green chiles and simmer together until the chiles are tender. Saute one-half pound of ground pork or beef which you have sprinkled with two teaspoons of oregano, one-half teaspoon garlic salt, one-half teaspoon of ground cumin and one-half teaspoon black pepper. Add the onions and garlic and saute. Then add the meat, onions, and garlic to the pot containing the green chiles and chicken broth. Simmer for 25 minutes. You do not have to add any thickening to the soup. Add salt to taste.

SANTA FE GREEN CHILE ENCHILADAS

There are never enough enchiladas in the world. Everyone loves them as they are great comfort food. I prefer using the 10-inch flour tortillas so the enchiladas will be huge, making everyone even happier.

8 green chiles (Anaheim or New Mexico-type)
2 fresh jalapeño chiles (if you like it hot)
2 cloves garlic, minced
1 and 1/2 cups chicken broth
1 and 1/2 teaspoons oregano
2 tablespoons flour
3 tablespoons water
1 cup sour cream
2 tablespoons oil
3 cups chopped onion (about 2 onions)
2 cups Monterey Jack, grated
1 cup Cheddar, grated

1. Char the large green chiles, remove the skins, seeds, and stems. Cut each chile into three pieces. Cut out the seeds and veins in the jalapeños.

2. Place all of the chiles in a saucepan with the broth, garlic, and oregano. Simmer for 20 minutes. Cool for a few minutes and then place the chiles, garlic, and a little of the broth into a food processor. Mince finely but do not puree. Place back in the saucepan with the broth. Make a paste using the flour and water. Stir into the chile broth. Simmer for about 10 minutes until thickened. Remove from the heat and stir in the sour cream. Set aside.

3. While chiles are simmering, you can saute the chopped onion in the two tablespoons of oil for 20 minutes, covering with a lid so they steam. The filling for your enchiladas will be sauteed onion, a little of the green chile sauce, and Jack cheese. When the onions are done, stir in one-third cup of the green chile-sour cream sauce. Set aside.

4. If you are using flour tortillas, you will need to heat them on a griddle to soften. It is not necessary to fry them. If you are using corn tortillas, place a couple teaspoons of oil at a time in a nonstick pan, and heat them just enough to soften.

5. Spread out one-half cup of sauce each in the bottoms of two long baking dishes. Place the softened tortilla on a flat plate and spread with a little sauce. Fill with one-fourth cup sauteed onion and one-fourth cup Jack cheese. Fold over the sides and place seam-side down in the dish. Spread green chile sauce over the top. Continue on making the rest of the enchiladas. Naturally, the flour tortillas will require more filling. Sprinkle the Cheddar cheese over the tops.

This recipe makes eight enchiladas if you use flour tortillas and about 12 if you use the corn tortillas. Bake for 15 to 20 minutes at 375 F. degrees or until the tops are golden. Do not overbake. Garnish with sprigs of cilantro.

NEW MEXICAN CHILES RELLENOS WITH BLUE CORNMEAL AND PINENUTS

I love the earthy taste of New Mexico's blue cornmeal ground from Blue Squaw corn and use it for baking and to roll green chiles in for one of the quickest methods of preparing rellenos.

6 to 8 fresh green chiles, Anaheim, Big Jims, or Sandias
1/2 pound Monterey Jack cheese, grated
1/4 cup pinenuts, lightly toasted
1/2 cup blue cornmeal
Evaporated milk, about 1/2 cup
About 1 cup light oil for frying

1. Char, skin, and remove seeds from chiles using your favorite method (See Chapter I).

2. Fit the combined cheese and pinenuts into the chiles.

3. Dip the filled chiles in the milk and then roll in the blue cornmeal.

4. Heat the oil in a deep frying pan and fry two chiles at a time until golden brown, turning over once. Drain on paper towels.

5. You can serve these New Mexican-style with Chile Colorado or Red Sauce. See page

CHILE NOTE: If you want to serve your chiles "Christmas" which is what the natives call anything served with a Red and a Green Sauce, ladle Chile Verde Sauce over your Rellenos along with the Red Chile Gravy.

SWEET CHILE ROLLS FOR CELEBRATIONS

In New Mexico, these little concoctions are usually served for weddings, holidays, and other festive celebrations when there are lots of people to feast on them. The first time I made these, using Big Jim chiles, my husband, our boys, and I consumed the entire platter. The sweet syrup traditionally served in northern New Mexico is very good poured over the tops of the chile rolls but we felt we could live without it. I serve the warmed sweet syrup in a side dish for those who want it.

2 pounds pork (I use pork chops)
6 fresh green chiles, New Mexican type or
    Anaheims
3/4 cup raisins
1/2 cup brown sugar
1 teaspoon cinnammon
1/4 teaspoon ground cloves
1/8 teaspoon or pinch nutmeg
1/4 to 1/2 cup pinenuts
1 egg, beaten

Batter:

1 cup flour for dredging chile rolls
4 eggs, separated
3 tablespoons flour
Light oil for frying

Sweet Syrup:

1/2 cup brown sugar
1 cup water
1/2 teaspoon cinnammon
1 teaspoon vanilla

1. Cover the pork chops with cold water and simmer for about one hour or until very tender. Cool in the broth.

2. Using a food processor, chop the meat.
Next add the chiles.
Chop to a fine texture so that the meat and chiles stick together. Next add the raisins. Chop. Place the meat-chile mixture in a bowl and stir in the spices and pinenuts. Add just enough beaten egg (you may only need one-half egg) so that the mixture sticks together. Form into small ovals.

3. Dredge the chile rolls delicately in the cup of flour (placed on a large piece of waxed paper.

4. Beat the yolks with the three tablespoons flour until thick and then whip the egg whites until soft peaks form. Fold the yolks into the whites.

5. Heat the oil in a deep frying pan and using a couple of spoons, dip each chile roll into the beaten eggs and lower into the hot oil. Fry until golden on both sides, turning over once. Drain on paper towels. Serve at room temperature as they are or serve with warm syrup.

6. Make the syrup by simmering the brown sugar and water for about 10 minutes. Stir in the cinnamon and vanilla.

VERA SANCHEZ' CHILE RELLENOS

These Chile Rellenos are made in a similar way to the Sweet Chile Rolls. They are an old family recipe done in the style of southern New Mexico. Also they make good use of chile pasado, the dried green chile. Vera serves these at family celebrations and as an appetizer. They freeze quite well.

1 pound ground sirloin
3/4 cup of reconstituted dried green chile
  (chile pasado)
1/2 cup chopped onion
2 cloves garlic, minced
4 ounces mushrooms, minced
  (Vera uses canned)
1 teaspoon salt
2 cups fine cracker crumbs (from Saltines)
5 eggs, separated
1 tablespoon flour
2 cups light oil for frying

1. Soak a heaping one-half cup of broken pieces of dried green chile in hot water for 1 to 3 hours before you plan to make the recipe.

2. Saute the ground meat, onion, and mushroms. Chop the soaked green chiles and add to meat. Saute for ten more minutes. Salt to taste.

3. Place the cracker crumbs on a plate. Separate the eggs and beat the yolks with the flour until thick and lemony. Whip the whites just until soft peaks form and fold the yolks into the whites.

4. Heat the oil. Stir about one-fourth cup of the egg batter into the meat mixture to help it stick together. Form a shape resembling a jalapeño chile. Place your chile on the cracker crumbs, holding it while you press on more crumbs, being careful that it doesn't crumble. It works, you just have to be gentle. Now lower your chile shape into the egg batter using a large spoon. Spoon more batter over the top. Next lower it into the hot oil, spooning more hot oil over the top to encourage puffing. When it is golden brown, turn it over. It takes about one minute on each side. Drain well on paper towels, blotting the top with paper towel.

The recipe makes about 30 to 35 chile rellenos.

LEROY'S MOTHER'S CALABACITAS

This is a kind of a squash stew, popular among the Indians, the Spaniards of California and in the Southwest. My husband loves it because he likes anything resembling slum-gullion. I just hope that someday when my boys grow up and do not recoil at green things, they will think of my squash like Leroy loves his mother's calabacitas. If you are thinking of becoming a vegetarian, this dish would convince you that you could survive on vegetables alone.

2 tablespoons oil or butter
2 cups chopped onion
6 or 7 green chiles, Anaheim, Big Jim, or
  Sandia, charred
1/2 cup water
1 pound zucchini
2 ears fresh corn (frozen or canned niblets
  are acceptable)
1/4 pound of Monterey Jack or Longhorn
  cheese, grated

1. Saute the onion in the butter until softened. Peel, seed, and remove stems of chiles. Chop into large pieces and add to the onions.

2. Add the water, the chopped zucchini, and the corn. Simmer for about 20 minutes. This dish is traditionally stewed until the squash breaks down and blends with the other ingredients. In that case, everything should be simmered at least 30 minutes. Toward the end of the simmering, sprinkle the cheese over the top.

DRIED RED NEW MEXICAN CHILES

All chiles start out green but when they are left on the vine during September and October, the timing is never exact, they turn a brilliant New Mexican red. A farmer is always courting with chance when he tries to achieve maximum ripeness in his chiles because an early frost can strike which results in bitter chiles.

Large groups of people assemble, sometimes entire families, to help farmers string the chiles into ristras which are hung up to dry slowly in the sun. By Thanksgiving time, the ristras will be dried. The red chiles are just as hot as the green but because they are a ripe fruit, they are sweeter than the green and that is why you will hear references to a particular dried chile (such as my favorite Dixon) having a lingering sweetness.

The dried chiles from New Mexico have incomparable flavor because they are SUN-DRIED rather than oven-dried. See Resources so you can have chiles shipped out-of-state. There is as great a variation among red chiles as there is among green so make sure of what you are getting. Since the milder green chiles, such as the Numex Big Jim are so thick and fleshy, they do not dry well. The hotter chiles, such as the Sandias and the Barkers, are not as meaty and dry very well so most of the time when you order dried red chiles from New Mexico, you will be obtaining the hotter varieties.

One of the most flavorful of the dried red chiles is the Dixon. It is sold ground-up into powder that could be called the Rolls Royce of ground chile but the cost is worth it. I use it in pots of chile and to make the quick chile gravy (chile colorado) that goes well over stacked enchiladas, chiles rellenos, and the Red Devil Potatoes.

The Dixon has such incomparable flavor, you do not need to doctor up the gravy as you sometimes do when you end up with tired, old chile powder.

One of the biggest complaints I hear from my cooking students is that the dried chiles or the chile powders they are using are hot and bitter. Often times, if a store does not turn over its chiles very rapidly, there may be quite a flavor loss due to old age or they may be purchasing chiles or ground chile from a source that dries the chiles at too high a temperature. Buy from a store that has high turnover in the ethnic section of their market or send away for your chiles.

RED DEVIL POTATOES
FOR BREAKFAST

Since we discovered these potatoes in Santa Fe, New Mexico, we do not let a week pass without having them for breakfast. The little restaurant where we enjoyed them piles a heap of potatoes in a wide soup bowl, covers them with red chile gravy (or chile verde), Jack cheese, chopped green onion, a fried egg if you like, and a little sour cream to help cool the mouth down. Since I love anything that's starch and anything with chile, these are my heaven and my downfall.

12 new potatoes (red-skinned), scrubbed
2 tablespoons oil
1/4 pound Monterey Jack cheese,grated
6 green onions, minced
1/2 to 3/4 cup sour cream
Red Chile Gravy, recipe below
Fried eggs for everyone, optional

1. Steam the potatoes for 20 minutes or parboil in two-inches water for 12 minutes.

2. When cool enough to handle, slice and chop the potatoes so they are irregular.

3. Using a heavy skillet, fry the potatoes until they are partly golden.This will take you about 15 minutes. While the potatoes are steaming or frying, you can stir up the Red Chile Gravy.

4. This recipe only serves four because every-one eats so much. To serve, fill four wide soup bowls with potatoes, pour over about one-

fourth cup Red Chile Gravy (but they'll want more), sprinkle on a little cheese, green onions, and a heaping tablespoon of sour cream. The fried egg is anticlimactic but give it to them if they want it.

RED CHILE GRAVY (to be used over any-thing)

2 tablespoons oil
1 tablespoon butter
2 tablespoons flour
1/4 teaspoons ground cumin
Scant 1/2 cup excellent, fresh ground red chile
    (like New Mexico Dixon)
1 cup cold water
2 to 3 cups chicken broth
    (canned is acceptable)
1 clove garlic, minced through press
Pinch of garlic salt

1. Heat the oil, stirring in the flour until it reaches a golden color. Add cumin. Mix the ground chile with the cold water until there are no lumps. Whisk it into the flour paste off the heat. Put back on the burner and slowly add the broth. Simmer for 15 to 20 minutes, stirring frequently. Add the garlic and garlic salt.

Simmer five minutes longer. Serve over the potatoes. This sauce will keep well for a week in the refrigerator. Use over enchiladas, chile rellenos, or burritos.

CHILE NOTE:

Use the above Red Chile Gravy over New Mexico-style Huevos Rancheros. Simply soften your corn tortillas in a little hot oil. Then cover them with grated cheese, some refried beans, a fried egg, and then envelop the whole affair in Red Chile Gravy.

CARNE ADOVADA

This spicy, marinated pork has a loyal following in New Mexico and is eaten there with great relish. It benefits from an overnight rest and freezes beautifully to later be used as they do in the Southwest, rolled up with pinto beans in a flour tortilla. Carne adovada is perfect for large parties because you can make it up in advance. You can prepare large pans of it and let people make up their own burritos.

The Red Chile Sauce:

*15 dried New Mexico chiles (or California
    dried chiles)*
4 pasilla or ancho dried chiles
4 cloves garlic, put through press
1 tablespoon Mexican oregano
1/2 cup chicken broth

The Meat:

3 and 1/2 pounds pork filet
1/4 cup apple cider vinegar

1. Rinse the chiles and pour boiling water over
them. Cover with a lid, allowing them to steep
for one hour.

2. Lift the soaked chiles out of the water and
place half of them at a time into a blender with
one-fourth cup water. Puree. Pour the puree
through a wire mesh sieve, pressing with a
spoon. Stir the garlic and oregano into this
puree and set aside while you prepare the meat.

3. Cut the pork into one-inch slices and then
into three-inch strips. Place in a glass or pot-
tery bowl and sprinkle with the vinegar. Next

envelop the meat with at least three-fourths cup of the chile puree. Marinate in refrigerator for a minimum of 12 hours or overnight.

4. Place the marinated pork with chile in a heavy cooking vessel covered with a double layer of foil or lid.   Bake at 325 F. for two hours. I use a Le Creuset, enameled cast-iron pot but a heavy roasting pan would work well.

5. Toward the end of the cooking, I mix the remaining chile puree (about one cup) with the chicken broth and pour it over the meat in order to create a thicker coating on the pork. Bake for at least 15 minutes longer. Serve Carne Adovada with piles of flour tortillas and beans so your guests can make their own burritos. This stores very well for three days in refrigerator. I also roll up burritos, wrap them in plastic wrap separately and store in freezer for instant snacks.

PURISTS' FIERY CHILE FOR COOK-OFFS

If I want to make friends with a chilehead or other stalwart soul, this chile is my choice. It was created by following a maxim issued by

67

Paul Prudhomme which is that complex tastes are created by a layering of sensations. All chiles are different and therefore each chile type delegated here hits your palate in a different region. This elixir maps out your palate into hit zones.

Also important is the necessity of scraping. With the advent of nonstick skillets, the true art of scraping is being culturally lost. Without frying and scraping, we would lose entire ethnic cuisines. Get out your cast-iron and fry the onions over medium heat until they turn a little golden and just begin to carmelize. Now you're ready to scrape the pan of the browned bits that are worth a king's ransom of spices. These pan scrapings can make the difference between a good chile and a great chile.

The addition of the Mexican chocolate is a secret weapon. A chile with too many jagged edges can be smoothed out with a little Ibarra chocolate.

*3 pounds of coarse chile-grind beef, ordered
  from butcher*
3 or 4 pork loin sirloin or chops
3-4 tablespoons oil for sauteeing ground meat

68

l can Mexican beer (Dos Equis preferred)
2 tablespoons oil for sauteeing onions
3 white onions, chopped
10 cloves garlic
2 cans Italian plum tomatoes with juice
   (1 lb., 12 oz. each)
3 tablespoons cumin seeds, toasted
2 or 3 tablespoons oregano, toasted
4 tablespoons ground ancho chile powder
   (may be labeled pasilla)
3 tablespoons ground California chile powder
4 tablespoons New Mexico chile powder
   (Chimayo preferred)
6 fresh Anaheim or New Mexican-type
   green chiles, charred and peeled
4-6 fresh jalapeño chiles, stems removed
   with some seeds
2 cans chicken broth
1/2 of a round of Ibarra Mexican chocolate
   (1 and 1/2 oz.) or substitute
2 tablespoons bitter cocoa powder and 1/4
   teaspoon cinnamon

1. In a heavy skillet, fry the onions over medium heat until they start to carmelize but stir
them around so they don't burn. Keep scraping
the pan! You may have to add more oil to the
pan.

2. Remove the fried onions from the skillet and fry the beef in two batches. Cut pork into small pieces. Drain off fat and add pork, beer, and all of the fried meat. Simmer for five minutes.

3. While everything is frying, roughly puree the plum tomatoes in a food processor, adding the garlic (cut into smaller pieces) so it gets minced. Do not liquidize the tomatoes. Set aside. Heat a small skillet and add the cumin seed and the oregano to toast. Keep stirring for two minutes. You'r finished when the cumin seed gives off a little puff of smoke and smells wonderful. Set aside.

4. You will need a 5 or 6-quart heavy pot to hold everything. To this
pot, add the fried beef, pork and beer, the sauteed onions, the toasted spices, the tomato-garlic rough puree, all of the red chile powders, and the chicken broth. Simmer for 40 minutes.

5. Meanwhile char the green chiles using your favorite method (Chapter I). Peel, seed, and stem. In the same food processor bowl used for the tomato puree (you didn't have to wash it), place the green chiles cut into pieces. Add the

jalapeños, which you have seeded and stemmed. Using an on and off pulse, chop all the chiles. You may use canned or dried chiles here instead of the fresh.

6. Stir the chopped chiles into the simmering pot of chile. Cook for 30 minutes. During the last 15 minutes, add the Mexican chocolate. Keep stirring to blend well.

As with all chiles, this one improves with a rest and freezes well. Do not even consider adding beans. It would be such a sacrilege, the pot would erupt and overflow onto the kitchen floor. Serve beans on the side.

CHILE NOTE:

One medium long dried red chile is equilvalent to one tablespoon chile powder. For homemade chile powder, break up dried chile and grind in clean coffee grinder. Whenever you see a chile powder with lots of yellow spots, it reveals the presence of ground up seeds.

CHAPTER III
POBLANO AND ANCHO CHILES

The poblano is a big, thick-fleshed, heart-shaped chile that I think of as the chile of Mexico and has been used there since before the arrival of the Spaniards. During the rainy season, from June to September, I remember stepping into areas of the marketplace in Querètaro and being overpowered by the aromatic fragrance of the just harvested sacks of poblanos. This wondrous, dark green chile is now, in the age of chile awareness, more available. Those poblanos grown in California are very mild in comparison to those from Mexico which we used to find so hot they would be given several warm saltwater baths before we could eat them.

With flame-charring, the crisp texture of the poblano changes to velvety meatiness and so it is one of the chiles that is most enhanced by roasting. It is also the chile most used for stuffing in Mexico. If the chiles you are using seem very hot (you will know because your eyes will begin to tear), soak them in warm water in which two teaspoons of salt have been dissolved. Add one/fourth cup vinegar. After 15 minutes, drain and use fresh water. Soak again for 10 minutes. This process will help a little but don't plan on it changing a hot poblano to a mild Anaheim. It will simply make the poblano less hot.

THE GREAT PASILLA HOAX

As I pursued the nomenclature of chiles during the research for this book, I came to the

74

conclusion that there was some kind of in-house Latin joke involving the naming of chiles. And everyone left to his own devices seemed to rename chiles according to where he was born, where his mother was married, or what neighborhood he lived in. Much of this injustice was and is all carried out in the name of the pasilla chile. Such capriciousness does not apply to the entire gamut of chiles, just mainly the pasilla. You are safer if you identify any chiles by looks rather than names.

WHAT REALLY IS A PASILLA? It is a poblano chile just as it has been called for centuries in Mexico but in parts of California, the poblano is called the pasilla. The poblano, when it has ripened, turned red, and is dried is called the ancho except in some parts of the West where it is erroneously called the pasilla. When you see pasilla ground chile powder in the market, they really mean ancho. The real pasilla chile is long (five inches), narrow, and chocolate-colored, lending its distinctive dark color to mole sauce. In some parts, the real pasilla is variously called the chile negro or the pasilla negro.

Charring and removing the skins of the poblano (pasilla): use any of the techniques mentioned in Chapter I. Since the poblano has a much thicker flesh than any other of the large chiles, it can be submitted to more heat during the flaming step and should be placed in a plastic bag to steam for 10 minutes before removing the skins. The poblano has a particularly large seed pod which you must reach in and pull out, playfully called castrating the chile in Mexico. The castrated or seeded chile is a capon (like a capon chicken).

CHILE RAJAS

Traditionally in Mexico it is assumed that when you refer to rajas, you mean strips of sauteed poblano chiles. The most common way to eat them is on the side of carne asada (grilled steak) with guacamole and tortillas. The sour cream and cheese mellow the chiles if you want to serve them over rice or pasta as a vegetarian dish.

Do not overcook your rajas, as their supreme
virtue is their fresh quality. If you do not have
poblano chiles, use any of the other large chiles
but do not use anything out of a can unless you
are trapped somewhere in the Arctic.

4 fresh large green chiles (poblano, Anaheim,
   New Mexican type)
2 tablespoons oil
1 tablespoon butter
1 onion, chopped
1 clove garlic, minced
1/2 cup to 1 cup sour cream
1/2 cup Monterey Jack or Italian Fontina
   cheese, grated

1. Char the chiles, remove skins, seeds, stems
and cut chiles into strips.

2. Meanwhile, saute the onion until golden
brown in the oil and butter. Then stir in the
garlic and strips of chile. Saute for about five
minutes.

3. If you are serving the Chile Rajas over the
top of grilled chicken or steak, you don't need
to add the sour cream. If you want to use the
Rajas over rice or in a tortilla, you can enrich

them by stirring in the sour cream and grated cheese. Just stir over the heat for one minute to warm. Remove from heat immediately and serve.

RAJAS WITH BROILED CHEESE

In this recipe I throw tradition to the wind and use a variety of chiles for Rajas instead of just poblanos. This dish makes a great appetizer but we never need dinner afterwards because we usually eat too much.

l pound of white cheese, grated (I use half
Italian Fontina for flavor and half Monterey
Jack or mozarella
2 cloves garlic, minced
2 fresh green chiles (poblano, Anaheim, or New
*   Mexico type)*
2 small chiles (jalapeño, Fresno, serrano), cut
*   into rings*
Tortillas, corn or flour

1. Grate your cheese and place in a heat-proof dish. I use my favorite blue and white Le Cruset oval dish.

2. Flame the large chiles until they are charred. Remove skins and seeds and cut into rajas or strips.

3. Mince the garlic. Sprinkle garlic over the grated cheese. Lay on the strips of chile and the rings of chiles. Place under broiler until cheese turns golden or place in hot 400 degree oven for about 12 minutes. The cheese should be crusty on top and liquid underneath. After removing from the oven you may sprinkle the top with snipped cilantro if you like. Serve to your guests as an appetizer with lots of hot tortillas. Everyone just takes a spoonful from the hot dish to his tortilla to his mouth.

GRILLED CHILES AND CHICKEN FILETS

Sometimes, when we make others happy by providing simplicity in all its glory, I wonder where we are all headed when we overcomplicate food. There are certainly days when I am happy with a bowl of soup or a freshly baked apple and my friends are incredibly happy when I give them this grilled dinner.

4 poblano (pasilla) chiles
3 whole chicken breasts, boned, skin removed
3 tablespoons olive oil
Juice of 2 fresh limes
2 cloves garlic, minced through press
1/2 teaspoon salt (optional)
Lots of freshly ground pepper
Fresh tortillas, flour or corn

1. Wash chiles and carefully cut down the sides so that you may reach in and pull out the seed pod. Wear gloves if you are sensitive to chile oil. Set chiles aside.

2. Place each chicken breast half between two sheets of wax paper and pound with a mallet just to flatten the chicken evenly. Place all of the pounded chicken in a long glass dish and cover with a marinade of two tablespoons olive oil, lime juice, garlic, salt, and pepper. Marinate at room temperature for 45 minutes.

3. Meanwhile, prepare your barbecue grill. The coals should be covered by a white ash and

the grill set at least six inches above the coals. Rub the remaining tablespoon of olive oil over the chiles so that they do not stick to the grill and place the marinated chicken on the grill.

The chicken needs about six to eight minutes per side. The secret is to keep turning the chicken and to grill the chiles until they are just a little cooked but still crisp. Keep turning the chiles. When everything is done to your satis- faciton (this only takes about 15 to 18 minutes) carry your platter to a cutting board. Cut the chicken into strips. Cut the caps off the chiles and discard. Cut the chiles into strips. Do not remove the chile skins. Toss the chicken and chile strips together and serve with hot tortillas and icy beer. Nothing else is needed.

FIESTA CHILES

Often in Mexico on Sundays, a friend who raised toros bravos (brave bulls) invited guests to his hacienda and staged little mock bullfights to the chagrin of gentler souls. We were im- plored to enter a small arena to practice our skills with a muleta while being chased by a baby bull and cheered on by the other guests hiding behind a wooden barricade. Once back in the hacienda courtyard we were rewarded by a great feast (or else I never would have appeared) accompanied by numerous arguments over who had the best verònica, one of the most elementary of the cape movements. Along with the usual barbecued goat, salsa, grilled maiz, and tortillas, there was always a platter of these stuffed chiles. Most of the eaters would typically fill a huge flour tortilla with barbecued strips of meat, salsa, and a hunk of chile relleno. This is Mexican ranch food at its best.

12 poblano chiles, charred, peeled, seeded
1 pound ground sirloin
1 pound ground pork (no seasonings)
1 cup chopped onion
1/2 cup tomato puree (from can)
1 potato, peeled, diced, cooked
2 carrots, peeled, diced, cooked
Salt and pepper to taste
6 eggs, separated
1 tablespoon flour
1/2 cup flour and wax paper
Light oil for frying

1. Fry the ground meats together until they have lost their pinkness and started to brown. Drain the pan of the fats and then stir in the onion. Saute with the meat until onion is softened. Stir in the puree, the cooked potato, and carrots. Season.

2. Place a scoop of the meat filling in each chile. Set aside

3. Prepare the batter by beating the egg yolks and flour until thickened. Whip the egg whites until soft peaks form and then fold the yolks and the whites together.

4. The oil should be heating in a deep frying pan. One inch of oil is plently. Using two forks lower a filled chile into the egg batter, place on a small dish and slide it into the oil. Spoon hot oil over the top and turn the chiles over once until both top and bottom are golden brown. Drain chiles on paper towels and blot them well.

5. As you continue on dipping chiles and frying, you will notice the batter getting soupy. Just whisk a little and it will revive.

6. You can serve these immediately or refrigerate them until needed and just briefly warm them for 10 minutes in a 350 degree oven. They are very good at room temperature which is how they are served in Mexico.

Serves eight to twelve people.

POBLANOS WITH CORN FILLING AND ANCHO SAUCE

Poblano chiles and corn are ancient friends and they are best paired in late summer and fall when each are in season. A California-style restaurant in Pasadena serves them grilled, without removing the skins, and bathed in a pungent Ancho Sauce.

6 poblano chiles, slit open, seeds removed
2 tablespoons light oil

1 cup corn kernels
2 tablespoons cilantro, snipped
1/2 cup mozzarela cheese, cubed
1/2 cup Italian Fontina or a sharp white
*   cheddar, cubed*
1/2 cup leftover poached or smoked chicken
*   (optional)*

1. Steam the corn kernels in a steamer basket over simmering water for only five minutes and then mix with the rest of the ingredients except the oil. Oil the surface of the chiles so they do not stick to the grill or the pan. Fill up the chiles and place over a medium hot gas grill or pan grill them in a heavy nonstick skillet for about 10 to 15 minutes until they soften a bit but still remain crisp rather than completely collapsed.

Serve as they are or in a pool of Ancho Chile Sauce.

ANCHO SAUCE

5 to 6 dried ancho chiles
1 tablespoon oil

1 tablespoon flour
1 clove garlic, minced
1/2 cup chicken or meat broth, more
  if necessary
Salt to taste

1. Rinse off the chiles, break up, discard stems and seeds. Place in heatproof bowl and add boiling water to cover the chiles. Place a lid over the bowl, allowing the chiles to steep for one hour.

2. Place soaked chiles in the blender with one-half cup water. Puree to a smooth texture. Pour the puree through a sieve, pressing with a spoon to force as much through the sieve as possible.

3. Heat oil in a skillet, add flour and stir until golden. Next add the chile puree, the garlic, and the broth. The broth is the secret to success. If you have wonderful homemade stock or juices left from roasting, your sauce will be exemplary. Simmer for 20 minutes. Add a pinch of cumin powder or oregano if you need to adjust flavors. Serve over your stuffed chiles or as a coating for enchiladas.

CHILE NOTE:

Some Latin leprechaun in the shape of an aunt or a grandmother has passed on the myth that within chile soaking water (and bean soaking water) lies all the flavor. Soaking water is culinary bathwater often containing field dust, grit, and bitterness. Throw it out and use fresh water or, even better, good broth or pan juices. The same old aunt, unavailable for comment at this time, probably said to take all your old vegetables from the icebox and make soup, resulting in "Old Tired, Moldy Vegetable Soup".

CHILES EN NOGADA, A NEW STYLE

During the autumn months in Mexico, when pears, walnuts, pomegranates, and poblano chiles are all in season, chiles en nogada are prepared in a classic style. I prefer to add more fresh fruit and no biznaga, the candied cactus which is frequently added to the filling and also I leave the chiles "naked", without a coating of

batter, so the walnut cream can be fully enjoyed.

6-8 poblano chiles (or fresh Anaheims)
1 pound pure ground pork (no seasoning)
1/2 cup chopped onion
1 clove garlic, minced
2 tomatoes
1 apple, peeled, chopped
1 pear, peeled, chopped
1 peach, peeled, chopped
1 tablespoon water
1/2 teaspoon cinnamon
pinch of ground cloves
1/4 cup raisins, blanched in hot water

1. Char the chiles over a flame, place in plastic
bag to steam for 10 minutes. Remove blackened skins, slit open chiles, and pull out seeds.
Try to keep the chile intact. Broil or bake the
tomatoes at 400 degrees for 15 to 20 minutes.
Lift the tomatoes out of any collected juice.
Cool slightly and blend in food processor.

2. Saute the ground pork. After it starts to
brown, remove some of the fat, and add the
onion and garlic. Saute for 10 minutes until

softened and stir in minced tomato. Saute to reduce some of the juice.

3. Add the chopped fruit and raisins. Simmer for five minutes longer but not until fruit is mushy. Stuff this filling into the prepared poblanos.

4. Place on an oiled baking sheet and bake for 10 minutes at 350 degress just to warm the chiles. Meanwhile prepare the Walnut Cream.

WALNUT CREAM:

1 package cream cheese, 8 ounces
1/3 cup milk
1/2 cup walnuts (or pecans)
1 pomegranate, red seeds removed for garnish

1. Place the cream cheese in food processor or blender and process until it is smooth and creamy. Add the milk a little at a time to create a sauce consistency and then add the walnuts and grind together just until nuts are minced.

2. Serve Walnut Cream over the filled, warm poblanos. Sprinkle a couple of teaspoons of pomegranate seeds over each chile.

POBLANO CHILE-CORN SOUP

Mexican soups are some of the best that you will find in any cuisine and much of the flavor can be attributed to the caldo. The chicken caldo usually has many wings, chicken backs, and of course a pair of cleaned chicken feet, the best part, my Mexican friends say. For color, they add brown onion skins along with a chopped onion, a roasted, unskinned tomato, and several cloves of garlic. Simmer for 2 hours and strain. Some of the chicken fat may be lifted off but not very much as this is the other secret to the rich, flavorful caldo. If you ask a Mexican cook for the caldo recipe, she will look at you like you are crazed. There is no recipe.

All you need is at least two and a half pounds of chicken parts, omitting the feet if you must, and a big five quart heavy pot. Cover the chicken with cold water. Add the onion skins, onion, roasted tomato, garlic, and salt to taste. Be inspired. And then use your caldo to make the soup below.

90

2 tablespoons oil or butter
1/2 cup chopped onion
3 tomatoes
2 cloves garlic, minced
3/4 cup corn kernels
1 poblano chile, charred, peeled, and chopped
1 quart of chicken caldo, preferably homemade
2 cups of water
Salt to taste
1/4 pound Monterey Jack cheese, cut into cubes

1. Saute the onion slowly in the butter. Meanwhile, roast the tomatoes under the broiler, turning often, for 15 minutes or roast in the oven for 20 minutes at 400 degrees. Cool for five minutes and then core the tomatoes and mince in a food processor or blender, skins and seeds included.

2. Place the caldo in a deep pot and add the sauteed onion, the minced tomatoes, the garlic, the corn kernels, and strips of chile. Simmer for 30 minutes. Taste and add salt if necessary.

3. Just before serving the soup, place five cubes of cheese in each soup bowl and ladle in the soup. The cheese will stay meltingly tender. Garnish with a couple of leaves of cilantro if you like.

CREAMY SWEET CORN SOUP

2 tablespoon butter
1/2 cup finely chopped onion
1 and 1/2 cups corn kernels
2 poblano or Anaheim chiles or
   1 can (7 ounces) green chiles, chopped
4 cups chicken broth
1 cup lowfat milk
1/2 cup cream

1. Char the chiles and remove skins and seeds. Chop. Saute onion in the butter until softened, about five minutes. Place one cup of the corn kernels in blender with one cup broth. Puree until smooth. In four-quart pot, put sauteed onion, chiles, pureed corn, the remaining broth, and corn kernels. Simmer for ten minutes.

2. Add the milk and cream. Do not boil the soup. Keep on low heat for five more minutes, just until soup is hot.

Creative addition:
Minced garlic, 1-2 cloves
Garnish of sour cream or creme fraiche

CORN AND CHILE PEPPER SALAD

The devotees of the produce grown by the
Chino family of Rancho Santa Fe will gladly
drive hundreds of miles for their white corn but
Susie Eisenmann and Dee Biller, cooking ex-
perts in the San Diego area, invented a salad
just to use THE WHITE CORN. Any other
fresh, sweet corn is almost as good and according to Susie, you should find every color of
chile possible to make a beautiful salad. But if
you don't buy your corn and chiles at the
Chino's, you will be missing the only vegetable
stand in the world that plays Vivaldi for back-
ground music.

Dressing:

2 teaspoons dijon-style mustard
2 cloves garlic, minced

1 to 2 tablespoons wine vinegar
1 tablespoon lime or lemon juice
1/3 cup olive oil
1/4 teaspoon freshly ground papper
1/4 teaspoon salt
2 tablespoons cilantro, snipped (optional)

Corn and peppers:

1 quart fresh white or yellow corn kernels
*6-8 assorted chiles and peppers-Anaheim, red
  and green bell peppers, poblanos, red and
  green jalapeños, fresnos*
1 red onion or handful of green onions

1. Blend all the ingredients for the dressing and set aside while you prepare the vegetables.

2. Steam the corn kernels for five minutes over simmering water.

3. Char and peel only the large chiles and peppers. Bell peppers have a wonderful sweet flavor when the translucent skin is removed by charring. You can even do this under a broiler because you will be cutting up the peppers and do not have to worry about keeping them intact.

4. Chop the onion or green onions. Remove the cores and seeds of the large peppers and cut into one-half inch strips. Remove the stems and cut out the seeds of the small chiles and mince.

5. Put all of the corn, chiles, peppers, onions, and dressing in a large glass bowl and toss. Serve at room temperature. This is a perfect salad for a picnic or summer barbecue.

Serves 8 to 10.

TORTILLA TORTE

This is sort of a Mexican lasagne done with flour tortillas. It is perfect for parties and large family gatherings. You can make it the day before you need it because the flavor improves with an overnight rest.

2 tablespoons oil
1 and 1/2 chicken breasts
Spice blend: 1 teaspoon ground chile, 1
 teaspoon oregano, 1 teaspoon ground
 cumin
1 can beer (12 oz.)
2 tablespoons oil
2 onions, chopped
1 package cream cheese (8 oz.)
1/2 cup black olives, halved
2 cups Cheddar cheese, grated
1 and 1/2 cups Quick Tomatillo Sauce
 (recipe below)
1 can green chiles, drained, cut into strips
6 flour tortillas (8 or 9-inch)
Springform pan (8 or 9-inch)
Butter or oil for pan

Quick Tomatillo Sauce:

2 cans tomatillos (13 oz.), drained
1 clove garlic
2 or 3 jalapeño chiles (canned is fine)
1 or 2 teaspoons vinegar

1. Blend the ground chile, oregano, and cumin
together and rub on skinned chicken breasts.

Brown on both sides in hot oil and then pour the beer over the chicken, place on a lid, and simmer for 20 minutes or until tender. Reserve the beer broth.

2. Saute the onion until golden brown and then add one-half cup of the reserved beer broth and simmer with the onions for a minute so that all of the brown bits are loosened. Using a large spoon, stir in the cream cheese in pieces just until blended. Do not overheat. Set aside.

3. Cut the chiles in thin strips. When the chicken is cool enough to handle, remove it from the bones and cut into crosswise strips.

4. Make the Quick Tomatillo Sauce by placing tomatillos in food processor along with the garlic (in pieces) and the chiles (in pieces). Puree to a sauce consistency. Taste and add more chiles if needed.

5. Oil the springform pan and begin the layering. Place one flour tortilla on the bottom and spread on about one-fourth cup of the cream cheese-onion, next add some chicken strips, some chile strips, a few olives, one-fourth cup

cheese, and one-fourth cup sauce. Repeat this layering until you place on the last tortilla. Cover this tortilla with the cream cheese mixture, some grated cheese, sauce, some strips of chile and olives all artistically placed. Bake at preheated 375 degrees for 35 minutes or until bubbly and golden. Let it set up for at least 15 minutes before serving.

6. To serve, run a sharp knife around the edge of the springform pan, release the sides, and lift the torte onto a serving platter using two wide spatulas. Use a thin, sharp knife to cut it into wedges.

Serves 8.

THICK TORTILLA SOUP

I was never happy slavishly cooking the classic tortilla soup with a few strips of fried tortilla floating in a caldo. I prefer the hearty, chunky tortilla soup like the one served at El Mirador in

San Antonio, Texas. As difficult as it was, I have tried to control myself long enough to stop improvising and write down this recipe. My cooking students have made it with great success so do not be discouraged by the banquet list of ingredients. Remember that chopping the myriad of vegetables is much easier than making puff pastry.

3 pounds of chicken parts or 1 whole
   chicken disjointed
3 quarts cold water
1 carrot, cut into pieces
1 onion, quartered
1 stalk celery with leaves, cut into pieces
3 or 4 green onion, cut into pieces
Handful of herbs (include parsley,
   sweet basil, cilantro)
2 teaspoons dried oregano
1 and 1/2 chicken breasts, skinned
1 large can Italian plum tomatoes
   (1 lb.12 oz), drained
3 dried ancho chiles(may be called pasilla)
1 onion, chopped
4 cloves garlic, minced
1 tablespoon oregano
1 or 2 teaspoons ground cumin
4 stalks celery, thinly sliced

1/2 cup corn kernels
1 large handful green beans, cut into
  1-inch pieces
1 and 1/2 cup sliced zucchini
4 carrots, peeled, sliced
3 new potatoes, skins on and diced
12 corn tortillas, cut with scissors into
  thin strips
1 cup light oil for frying strips
1/2 pound fresh spinach or fresh sorrel
1 or 2 Hass avocados (not overripe!), cubed
1/2 cup cilantro, snipped
1 pound Monterey Jack cheese, grated

1. This recipe looks long but it can be done in stages. Actually, the longest part is cutting up vegetables. If you make the broth and fry the tortilla strips the day before you want the soup, you will sail through the rest.

2. To make the broth, rinse the chicken parts, place in six quart heavy pot, and cover with cold water. Bring to simmer and for the first 20 minutes you will need to skim off foam. Then allow the pot to simmer partially covered for two hours. Add nothing else.

3. Now remove the chicken parts. Give the overboiled chicken meat to the dogs and throw away the bones. Strain the broth. You may refrigerate it overnight or continue on. If you refrigerate the broth do not remove ALL of the congealed chicken fat or you will lose flavor. Just remove some of the fat unless you are following strict dietary restrictions.

4. Put the broth back in the large pot. Add the carrot, celery, onion, all of the fresh herbs, green onion, dried oregano, and the three breast halves. Bring this all to a quiet bubbling and simmer gently for 30 minutes. **THIS IS THE IMPORTANT PART TO THIS SOUP.** The flavor of the vegetables and fresh herbs is given up to the broth instead of being boiled away as is done in many stocks.

5. After 25 minutes, be sure to remove the chicken breasts so they are not overcooked.

6. While your pot is simmering above, you can do the rest of the work. Rinse off the dried chile pods and break them into pieces. Cover with boiling water and let them steep for 20 minutes. Place them into the blender with one-

half cup water. Puree. Push this puree through a mesh sieve to strain out the chile skins.

7. Put the chile puree into a food processor bowl or blender along with the canned plum tomatoes, the garlic, the onion, oregano, and ground cumin. Puree this mixture together. Set aside.

8. Remove the cooked vegetables and herbs from your simmered broth using a strainer. Discard the cooked vegetables and herbs. Now stir the chile-tomato mixture into the broth and simmer while you chop vegetables.

9. Add the chopped and diced vegetables to the broth (everything but the chicken, tortilla strips, fresh spinach, avocados, cheese, and cilantro). Simmer the soup for 30 minutes.

10. Fry the tortilla strips until golden and crisp in hot oil. Drain well on paper towels. Set aside for serving time.

11. Wash and dry the spinach or sorrel. Cut into strips using a sharp knife or scissors.

12. Remove the cooled breast meat from the bones and cut into cubes.

13. During the last 10 minutes stir in the chicken cubes and all but one cup of the spinach.

14. You may save the soup for several hours, a day, or serve immediately. To serve, place a handful of fried tortilla strips in large, wide soup bowls and ladle in the chunky soup. Sprinkle three tablespoons grated cheese over the top and garnish around the edges of the bowl with snippets of spinach or sorrel. Pass cilantro for those who cannot live without it. This soup is a banquet and needs little else to accompany it unless you are gluttonous enough to require dunking bread and a glass of wine.

Serves eight.

DRIED ANCHO CHILES

The ancho chile is the most loved dried chile of Mexico. It has a rich sweetness that, when used in combination with the other dried chiles, can mellow their ascerbic qualities. As discussed earlier in The Great Pasilla Hoax, you might find it in markets labeled as pasilla. Ancho means wide so look for a wrinkled, plump, wide chile whatever it is labeled. It is often confused with the mulato chile which is also wide and plump. But the ancho is reddish-brown and the mulato is blackish-brown or achocolatado, meaning chocolate colored. This slight difference in coloring is most evident when the chiles are held up to the light. The ancho is one of the most important chiles in classic mole sauces.

CHICKEN MOLE ENCHILADAS

About three times a year, we make the trip from our mountain town to the Grand Central Market in Los Angeles so I can buy my mole chiles and when I concoct the mole, the same scenario ensues. I cannot believe how good it is. It is always different each time, sometimes hotter, sometimes richer. And I chastize myself for not making it more often. These Chicken Mole Enchiladas are just one more excuse for eating the seventh wonder of Mexican cuisine.

3 dried ancho chiles

4 pasilla negro chiles (narrow and
  chocolate-colored)

4 California or New Mexican type dried chiles

2 tomatoes, charred or roasted

1/4 cup pecans, toasted

1/4 cup almonds, toasted

2 cloves garlic, toasted in skins

3 tablespoons raisins, blanched in hot water

1/2 teaspoon cinnamon

1 and 1/2 cups chicken broth, reserved
  from cooking

1 round Ibarra chocolate (3.1 oz.)

1/2 ripe banana (eat the other 1/2)

1 and 1/2 chicken breasts, skinned

2 cans chicken broth for cooking

2 tablespoons oil

1 onion, chopped

12 corn tortillas

1/4 pound Monterey Jack cheese, cut into sticks

1. Wash the chiles off in cold water. Break them open and shake out most of the seeds and remove stems. Wear thin gloves if you are sensitive to chile oil. Place chiles in a large bowl, cover with boiling water, place on a lid, allowing chiles to steep for one hour.

2. Meanwhile place the chicken in the broth and simmer for 25 minutes. Remove chicken and when cool enough to handle, pull meat off the bones and shred. Place in refrigerator until you finish sauce.

3. Toast the nuts in a 350 F. degree oven for about 10 minutes. Toast the unpeeled garlic in the same pan.

4. When the chiles have soaked an hour, place a few at a time into a blender with about one-fourth chicken broth reserved from cooking. Puree chiles adding a little hot water if needed to facilitate blending. Puree each batch of the soaked chiles with some chicken broth. Add the tomatoes and garlic to the last batch and puree along with the chiles. Pour all of the chile-tomato-garlic puree through a wire strainer to strain out skins and seeds.

5. In a blender combine half of the strained puree, the toasted nuts, raisins, cinnamon, and banana half. Puree.

6. Place the mole sauce into a high-sided five-quart saucepan, add the round of chocolate, and simmer for 30 minutes.

7. While the mole is simmering, saute the chopped onion in oil until translucent. Mix the onion with the shredded chicken which will serve as the enchilada filling. Using the same skillet, saute each corn tortilla in a couple teaspoons of hot oil just until softened. Place one-half cup of mole sauce at a time in a plate. Lay the tortilla in the plate and turn to coat it with sauce. Place filling on the tortilla and roll up. Arrange the enchilada in the baking dish and continue filling and rolling. Garnish the top of each enchilada with one stick of cheese. You can thin out the mole sauce, if necessary, with more chicken broth and spread it over the enchiladas just before baking. Serve more warm mole at the table.

8. Bake enchiladas from 15 to 20 minutes at 350 degrees.

CHAPTER IV
SMALL CHILES
JALAPEÑOS, SERRANOS, FRESNOS,
GUEROS

I have never encountered a mild, small chile.
The smaller the chile, the greater the concentration of capsaicin. At the same time, these
chiles invite the greatest passion and although
no one is said to have died from an overdose of
8-Methyl-N-vanillyl-6-nonenamide or capsaicin, its absence in the diet of devotees has
caused terrible bouts of homesickness in distant

parts of the world and withdrawal symtons in those who thought they could live without it. After an evening out enjoying a delicate French dinner, I probably would not consciously state that I am yearning for some 8-Methyl-N-vanil-lyl-6-nonenamide but the next morning, as predictable as the swallows returning to Capis-trano, I am eating hot salsa over my eggs for breakfast.

JALAPEÑO CHILE: This little chile, a favorite in California and Texas, is almost ten times hotter than the mild Anaheim. It has the distinction of being the only chile smuggled into space on board the *Columbia..* The jalapeño has so pervaded the culture, it could be called the chile of forty-one flavors. It can be found in ice cream, lollipops, Cajun martinis, and it still remains my favorite salsa chile. I love the bright, just-right hotness and crisp texture.

Even though the jalapeño is the thickest-walled of the small chiles, it is very tender when fresh and charring it is unnecessary unless you want that particular smoky flavor. To avoid burning my hands with capsaicin (chile oil) when I am working with jalapeños, I slice the chile in half and then use a very sharp paring knife to cut against the inner walls of the chile, releasing the seed pod and the veins. It is important to let the knife do the work, not your fingers. Then I put all the chile halves on a cutting board and cut them into quarters. If I am chopping a large amount of chiles, I put them into the food processor and mince them with on and off pulsations. For one or two chiles, I use a large chef's knife for fast mincing and then wash my hands very well afterwards. I suffered many an evening of chile burns on my hands before I allowed my trusty food processor to do the job. If you are extremely sensitive to chile oil, you must protect your hands with thin surgical gloves and use your food processor and sharp paring knife as much as possible to avoid direct exposure to chile innards.

FRESNO CHILE:

The Fresno is frequently the same size as the jalapeño but a lighter green. It seems to only be available in the chile season from July to November. Watch for red Fresnos in the fall months. Some cooks prefer the Fresno because they think it is a little sweeter and less sharp than the jalapeño. This gesturing is like a comparison of Granny Smith to Pippin apples and depends on your personal tastebuds. The Fresno is just as hot as the jalapeño so use it for the same recipes. Never available canned.

GUEROS (pronounced where-ohs):
These chiles, a great favorite of Mexican cooks, are the same size as the jalapeños and Fresnos and about the same heat level. They are a yellow white color wherefore springs their name - the blondes. If you are called a "guero" in Mexico, that is an affectation referring to your light color. The gueros are the fall-winter-spring chiles. They are almost always available fresh but unlike the ubiquitous jalapeños, they are never available canned. The gueros are very thin-walled which is why I think the Mexican cooks like them. They toast them in a skillet until the skin is charred and loosened and then they grind them on a molcajete (seeds and veins included) so the chiles can be easily blended into a hand-chopped salsa cruda. This operation is not easy with a jalapeño because of the thicker flesh.

SERRANO:
The little two-inch long, half-inch wide serrano is definitely hotter than the aforementioned

chiles. The serrano is well-loved by Mexicans and those aficionados who have passed several tests of survival. I use it in combination with other chiles or when I need a very hot salsa for fire-eaters and believe me, they are out there in growing numbers. The serrano is a little more difficult to find unless the market is catering to a nearby Mexican population. I have found it most often in Latin grocery stores and vegetable stands. Do not buy serranos if the stems are black and dried, a sign of old chiles. The Mexicans slice the serrano into little rings (do not remove seeds or veins for this) for their salsa cruda. The shock is awe-inspiring but good.

THAI CHILE:

 when fresh this chile is about four inches long and barely a half-inch wide. When I found them for the first time in the Sunday San Jose Flea Market, the Thai vendor repeatedly warned me against them. When I asked him if he liked them, he gave me a shocked "No!!!! Too hot!" Somebody must be using them because his stall was overflowing with these chiles resembling little green snakes.

SMALL DRIED RED CHILES

Some small chiles are never available in their fresh, green state and are only found in the United States when dried.

CHIPOTLE CHILES: these are dried jalapeños which can be smoked over a variety of things, from mesquite to oak to banana leaves, depending on where they are from. They are difficult to find, just simply dried and smoked, unless you send away for them or go to a Latin market. They can be black or a greyish white depending upon their treatment but their wonderfully complex, hot flavor has made them one of my favorite chiles when used with discretion as they can overpower if they are used in too great a number. Look in the ethnic sections of supermarkets to find them canned en adobo, a vinegary sauce. These will keep for several months if refrigerated in a glass jar and are a great addition to beans, stews, and blended with olive oil and garlic, they are good rubbed onto pizza dough before baking. See Chapter V.

DRIED RED JALAPEÑOS: ripe, red jalapeños are available in some Latin markets and vegetable stands during the fall months. Dried, red jalapeños are available by mail order. Last summer, I very successfully dried red jalapeños in the sun under cheesecloth and finished drying them for a day in my dehydrator. I grind them up in the electric coffee mill relegated to spices and mix them with home-grown oregano and cumin seeds, dried onion flakes and garlic to make my own Southwestern spice mix. I was surprised to read in some resource books that the only way of drying jalapeños is by smoking which I have found to be untrue. In fact, the little vegetable stand I frequent is now quite colorful with an array of red jalapeños strung out and drying in the desert sun so drying potential of any chile depends upon enviornment.

CASCABEL: little round brick-red chiles aptly named "jingle bells" because of their rattling seeds. They are moderately hot with a nutlike flavor. Difficult to find unless you go to a Latin market. Mexicans like to add them to salsas.

CHILES DE ARBOL: these are hot and very similar to the japones chiles. They are frequently available in cellophane packets in the ethnic sections of supermarkets. They can be toasted in a skillet, ground up, and put in salsas. Very hot.

GUAJILLO (prounounced wa-he-yo): a orangish-red chile about three inches long, usually available only in Latin markets. Considered hot but with sweet overtones. Mexicans use it in sauces in combination with other chiles. It is a favorite in Mexico and pre-Columbian in origin.

CHILE PEQUIN (pronounced pay-keen): comes in the shape of light red seeds and is harvested by the Indians in Mexico and along the border where entire families will cooperate in the tedious picking of these miniscule, potent chiles which grow wild and uncultivated. They are expensive and so of great value in northern Mexico. A little bit goes a very long way. New Mexicans like using them in salsas. Very, very hot.

JAPONES (pronounced ha-po-naise): skinny, very hot chiles often sold in cellophane

packets in supermarkets and claimed to be
dried, red serranos although there is no proof of
this. These chiles can be used interchangeably
with with chiles de arbol or in place of the
pequins if you want them extremely hot. The
japones chile is used in both Chinese stir-fry
and in some Italian dishes, being left whole as
the dish is being cooked.

THE FASTEST SALSA IN THE WEST

Even though I compiled and tested many salsa
recipes for *The Salsa Book*, I never stop
searching for just one more salsa. Different
cooking techniques used with the same ingredients can produce vastly different results.

While reading an old Mexican cookbook, I
discovered that Latin cooks sweeten their tomatoes by briefly roasting them. They pour off the
juices, which they feel contains the acid, and
grind them, skins and all. In *Cuisines of
Mexico,* Diana Kennedy recommends broiling
the tomatoes for the same effect. Since I have

a restaurant stove lacking a broiler, I found it necessary to oven- roast the tomatoes You puree the whole tomato without the bother of skinning or seeding and the resultant salsa is a brilliant red.

This technique works best if you are using ripe, red tomatoes from a reliable source like your garden, a stand, or a market that hasn't waxed the skins. I am particularly excited about this salsa because it not only tastes superb but it saves the cook time.

3 pounds of ripe, red tomatoes, washed, halved
4 cloves garlic, minced through press
3-6 jalapeño chiles, stemmed, seeded
1/2 cup white onion, minced
2 tablespoons fresh ground chile powder (New Mexico)
1/4 teaspoon ground cumin
Garlic salt or salt to taste
1/4 cup apple cider vinegar

1. Preheat oven to 400 F. degrees and roast tomato halves in pyrex dish (you may need two) for 20 minutes. Set aside to cool. There will be clear juices in the bottom of the dish. Discard.

118

2. In two batches, place the cooled tomato halves in your food processor or blender and roughly puree. Do not overprocess the salsa. Add pieces of the jalapeños during the processing of the second batch. Chop using short pulsations.

3. Using a wide four-quart saute pan, simmer the tomato puree, chiles, garlic, onions, chile powder, cumin, and apple cider vinegar. After 10 minutes of simmering over medium heat, give it the taste test. Add more of any one of the chiles, spices, or garlic salt if needed. I purchase a superb ground chile from New Mexico called Dixon chile caribe (see Resources at back of book for address). This particular chile adds so much flavor (not just heat), I am astounded that I have put up with lesser chile powder all these years. Incidentally, chile caribe is the New Mexican term for coarsely ground chile including all of the seeds.

4. Your salsa is ready for eating or storing in glass jars in the refrigerator. Use it over everything and in particular huevos rancheros. Makes about one and a half quarts.

FAST AND EASY MEXICAN GREEN SAUCE

One of the greatest accomplishments of authentic Mexican cooking is the green sauce made from tomatillos when everything is done right. The tomatillos must be cooked just a little to pale their lemony bite. When you see tomatillos in the market, they are covered by a dry membrane. Peel this membrane back to make sure they are a bright lime green, not yellow. Yellowish tomatillos are old and taste terrible.

There is a taco stand in Van Nuys which has the best green sauce. They would not tell me one small clue but the manager unwisely sold me a cup of the stuff and after analyzing it under my culinary microscope I came up with an exact duplicate. I love a challenge!

2 pounds tomatillos
3 serrano chiles or 4 jalapeños
2 cloves garlic, minced through press
1/2 bunch of washed and dried cilantro
1 teaspoon vinegar
Salt to taste

*1/4 pound Monterey Jack cheese, cubed
   (optional)*
1 ripe but firm avocado, cubed (optional)

1. Wash the tomatillos off in warm water and
remove the dry membranes. Rinse off some of
the sticky residue.

2. STEAM the tomatillos and the whole
serranos for four minutes. Cool.

3. Cut open the chiles and, using a small knife,
cut out some of the seeds and veins. Mexican
cooks would not do this but would use the
whole serrano. Cut serrano into pieces. Place
tomatillos and serranos into food processor or
blender. Puree roughly and then add the garlic
and cilantro. Puree to a finer texture. Add
vinegar and salt to taste.

4. Use Mexican Green Sauce on California
Tortilla Pizza, enchiladas, burritos, nachos or if
you want it for dipping large tortilla chips, stir
in the cubes of cheese and avocado.

MAGIC JALAPEÑO JUICE

Sometimes you taste a salsa or dressing that needs an infinitismal something. This magic juice is it. It has been variously called "jalapeño hots", "hot licks", and conservatively "instead of salt". It all came about because I used the juice from the canned jalapeños en escabeche as much as the jalapeños themselves. You can add magic juice to your salsa, tuna, salad dressing, stews, guacamole, or your marinades particularly for fajitas. Keep it in the refrigerator for emergencies. Make it your replacement for salt if you are on a restricted diet.

6 jalapeños (or more)
1 cup water
2 cups apple cider or white vinegar
2 tablespoons olive oil
3 cloves garlic, smashed
1/2 teaspoon oregano
1 slice of onion
1 teaspoon peppercorns, smashed

1. Poke the chiles in a couple of places with a

122

sharp paring knife. Place everything in a saucepan and simmer for five minutes. Cool and
place in a glass jar or bottle. Use with little or
no discretion.

CHILE NOTE:
When a salsa recipe calls for vinegar or lime
juice, use a little Magic Jalapeño Juice.

NEW MEXICAN SALSA

On the West Coast, they like chunky salsa on
the mild side and in New Mexico, they like it
thinner and much hotter. The fiery pequin chile
used in this salsa does the trick.

2 cups tomato juice (Sacramento is good
brand)
1 teaspoon crushed chile pequin
1 teaspoon Mexican oregano
2 cloves garlic
1/2 to 1 teaspoon fine black pepper
1 teaspoon sugar
Pinch of ground cumin
1 teaspoon vinegar
1/4 cup minced white onion
1/2 cup minced tomato, seeded and skinned

1. Place one cup of the tomato juice in a blender with the chile pequin. Blend well.

2. In a saucepan, combine the tomato juice-pequin mix, rest of juice, minced garlic, the oregano, pepper, sugar, cumin, and vinegar. Simmer for five minutes. Stir in the minced onion and tomato. Cool mixture. Use for dipping tostada chips. This salsa will thicken quite a bit after refrigeration.

SALSA CRUDA

There are a hundred variations of these salsa in every village of Mexico, depending upon what chiles are grown in the local area. I have had guests go through mountains of this salsa which goes to prove that everyone is hungry for freshness and it doesn't have to be complicated.

4 ripe, red tomatoes
1/2 cup diced white or red Bermuda onion
2 fresh serrano or jalapeño chiles
1 or 2 pickled jalapeño chiles

1/2 cup cilantro, snipped
Salt to taste
Lime juice or Magic Jalapeño Juice

1. Remove core of tomatoes, cut in half horizontally, and gently squeeze out seeds and some juice.

2. Dice tomatoes and onions about same size.

3. Remove chile stems and cut open chiles. Cut out most of veins and seeds. If you were in Mexico, you wouldn't do this. Leave some seeds for authenticity. Mince the pickled chiles.

4. Stir everything together. Taste and add a squirt of lime juice or the Magic Jalapeño Juice to your taste. Serve within a hour. This is not the salsa to make in the morning for the evening dinner. Salsa Cruda must be absolutely fresh as a salad. At times, I replace the vinegar or lime juice with balsamic vinegar (the less aged, less expensive kind) and that can also be wonderful. Serve Salsa Cruda with grilled foods or traditional Latin meals.

FIREMANS' SALSA

During the course of numerous book signings
and salsa tastings for *The Salsa Book*, one of
the most predominant occupational groups to
show up for these events were firemen and they
kept telling me that my salsa wasn't hot
enough. In honor of my next local book sign-
ing, I decided to meet the challenge and make
the hottest salsa I had ever made. It passed the
test.

3 pounds tomatoes
1 bunch of green onions, minced using part of
  green tops
1/2 cup minced white onion
6 jalapeño chiles, stems and some seeds
  removed
6 serrano chiles, minced (including everything)
4 jalapeños en escabeche, minced with seeds
1/4 cup jalapeño juice from can or Magic
  Jalapeño Juice
2 cloves garlic, minced through press
1 tablespoon olive oil
1/2 cup cilantro
Salt to taste

1. Blanch tomatoes in boiling water for 30 seconds to loosen skins Hold under cool water to cool. Remove skins. Cut tomatoes in half horizonally and squeeze to remove most of seeds and some juices. Chop.

2. Combine tomatoes with the rest of ingredients. This salsa can be made several hours before you need it at the firehouse so the flavors blend. If you want it hotter, add more chiles.

Note: if it is winter time and tomatoes are pink golfballs, just use two large cans of Italian plum tomatoes, drained of juice, and squeezed to remove seeds and water. Add two or three fresh tomatoes for the texture.

EAST L.A. SALSA

If you love real Mexican food as we do, you learn that the best places to find it are the family-run restaurants in Mexican neighborhoods. As soon as you sit down at our favorite place, they bring you a plate of freshly fried totopos (corn tortilla triangles), sprinkled with shreds of a sharp white cheese and a bowl of warm, mahogany-colored salsa like nothing you have ever tasted. It is deliciously picante and at the same time so exotic, I can imagine this salsa being eaten in Mexico centuries ago. I give this salsa to the same friends who love mole. In fact, the salsa is the same achocolatado (chocolate) color of mole due to the addition of the almost black pasilla negro chiles. The Mexican chef would only tell me the four chiles that he used and that he toasted them to bring out the flavor. The rest was a lot of lunches in East L.A. until I got the salsa right.

4 guajillo chiles (dried)
4 pasilla negro chiles (dried)
6 California chiles (dried)
6 cascabel chiles (dried)
1 and 1/2 cups water
1 clove garlic
pinch of ground cumin
pinch of oregano
2 teaspoons vinegar
1/4 teaspoon salt or more to taste

1. If the dried chiles are dusty rinse them off and then lightly toast them in a heavy skillet. Keep turning them over and over for about 2 or 3 minutes until they soften. Do not burn them or they will be bitter. Don't worry about toasting the cascabels because they roll around in the pan too much.

2. Run cool water over the toasted chiles and break them open to remove the seeds and stems. Place in a bowl and cover with boiling water. Add the garlic to the water. Steep for 15 minutes just to soften them a little.

3. Place the soaked chiles and garlic in a blender jar and cover with one and a half cups of fresh water. Puree until smooth. Add the cumin, oregano, vinegar, and salt to taste.

4. This salsa should be served warm and is best over freshly fried tortilla strips or triangles or a good brand of tostada chips, unadulterated by too much salt or nacho seasonings. I sprinkle my chips with shreds of Italian Fontina or Monterey Jack and drizzle the warm salsa over the tops.

THE MAGIC OF CHIPOTLES

CHAPTER V

With their sudden, meteoric rise in popularity, you would think that the chipotle is a new chile, some phenomenal hybrid whipped up in Las Cruces to appease our appetites for hotter and hotter stuff. But chipotle chiles have been around since ancient times in Mexico. They are simply jalapeños preserved by a smoking process. The Aztecs utilized the process of

131

smoke-drying in deep pits or caves in order to pre-
serve thick-walled chiles which do not easily air dry
even when strung in ristras. Preservation by smoking
works especially well in damp climates prone to long
rainy seasons.

As a result of smoking, the chiles change color,
becoming a whitish tan or retaining a deep red such as
the morita or mora, a type of smoked chile found in
Oaxaca. The smoking process seems to make chiles
more fiery and complex. The deep flavors of the
chipotle and mora unfold upon your palate in waves
and then are quickly gone, minutes later.

WHAT TO DO WITH CANNED
CHIPOTLE CHILES:

Canned chipotles en adobo are found in the ethnic
sections of supermarkets and in Mexican grocery
stores. The adobo sauce is made up of tomato puree,
vinegar, salt, and sugar. Because they are very soft
and moist, the canned chipotles are the easiest to use.
Remove any stems and most of the seeds and place
the chiles and their adobo sauce in the bowl of a food
processor. Puree to a smooth paste. Place in a clean
glass jar. This chipotle paste will keep for a couple of
months in the refrigerator and you can easily blend it
into sauces whenever you need it.

132

WHAT TO DO WITH DRIED CHIPOTLE OR MORA CHILES:

Dried chipotles can be ground into a powder and then mixed with other milder ground chiles such as ancho or California, ground dried garlic, kosher salt, herbs and spices

The best way to grind up the tough, dried chipotles is with an electric coffee grinder. The grinders made specifically for spices do not seem to work as well with dried chiles.

The morita chiles from Oaxaca, the whitish tan chipotles found in most Mexican stores, and the mora chile (sometimes mistakedly called chipotle) can be used interchangeably. The chiles are extremely hot so it is difficult to taste the fine nuances that may exist.

The spice blend below is good rubbed on chicken, turkey, pork, or steaks but it is equally good on vegetables. I place wedges of winter vegetables brushed with olive oil in an oiled deep pan holding about 1/2 cup water or broth. Sprinkle with the spice blend and bake covered for thirty minuts. . Then remove cover and continue baking ten more minutes so vegetables may brown. It is best to turn them once or twice. Wedges of yam are especially good and their sweetness and the chipotle marry well.

CHIPOTLE SPICE BLEND

1 tablespoon ground dried chipotle chile
2 tablespoons chile powder (like Dixon or other New
  Mexican chile)
1 teaspoon salt
1 tablespoon dried oregano, rubbed
1 teaspoon ground dried garlic

1. Snap off the stems and break up the chiles. Place in the well of the coffee grinder. If the chiles are small, you will need to use about five or six. If using large chipotles, you will need about three. Grind into a rough powder with some texture.

2. Mix all the rest of the ingredients together.

The spice mixture can be blended in huge amounts or you can add some of your own favorite spices like ground cumin, black pepper, paprika, or another type of chile. Use the salt at your own discretion but it serves to appease the hotness of the chiles and actually brings out their flavors. Store spice blend in a glass jar.

Another way to use the spice blend is to mix it with

lime juice, beer, or wine along with a little olive oil. Use this for a marinade. Use one tablespoon spice blend to one-half cup liquid.

Dried chipotles or mora chiles can be covered in boiling water. Soak for one hour. Puree, strain, and use just as you do the canned chipotle puree.

CREAMY CHIPOTLE SAUCE

This sauce was made up in heaven to rescue tostadas from boredom. A tostada is basically a salad on top of a crisp tortilla or a salad mixed with bits of toasted tortilla wedges. You can add cherry tomato halves, shredded chicken, olives, grated cheese and salsa. Or in place of salsa, drizzle Creamy Chipotle Sauce over the top of the tostada.

1/4 cup mayonaise
1/2 cup nonfat or lowfat plain yogurt
Juice from 1 lime
1 clove garlic minced through press
1 canned chipotle chile, pureed
1/4 teaspoon salt

1. Blend all of the above ingredients in a food processor. Do not add more chiles until you taste the heat level.

Makes about 3/4 cup to serve as a dressing for sandwiches, tostadas, or tortas. This sauce can even be spread over bread slices before making a grilled cheese sandwich. Spectacular!

TORTAS
MEXICAN SANDWICHES

A torta is the Mexican version of a Dagwood, the architectual wonder of all sandwiches. It is everything good balanced between two pieces of bread. Definitively speaking, the bread should be a bolillo or a crusty Italian roll.

If you hesitate momentarily and try to look too civilized while you are eating a torta, you are likely to lose parts of it on the sidewalk. In Mexico City, eating tortas ranks as a sidewalk extracurricular activity. Even if you're full, you can't pass a good torta man. A torta vendor is judged by his extras. Does he have pickled onions or just raw onion slices.? Is his chicken roasted, grilled, or simply boiled? Does he put on a thin tasty layer of refried beans? Can you have salsa or sliced tomatoes. Are there pickled serrano chiles or pickled chipotles? And on and on into infinity The best tortas have many layers of flavors.

136

For a summer patio party, I like to load a picnic table with several filling ingredients and a basket of bolillos, teleras, or baguettes cut into manageble lengths for tortas. Let the guests have at it and construct their own tortas. All you need is beer, wine, or aqua fresa.

MEXICO CITY TORTA

Our favorite vendor in Mexico used spiced chicken rather than the soggy, boiled chicken used by many other vendors. His bolillos were particularly good because they were crustier on the outside with a creamy interior, hinting at a spice we never figured out (which I now think was cinnamon). A true bolillo is pointed at the ends and has a crack on top. Round telera rolls are softer and can also be used for tortas but you can easily substitute French or Italian rolls.

For six people:

6 bolillos or crusty Italian rolls
1 and 1/2 pounds boned chicken breasts
 or turkety tenderloins
1 tablespoon olive oil
3 tablespoons lime or lemon juice
2 cloves garlic, minced through press

1/2 teaspoon salt
1/4 teaspoon pepper
1/4 pound queso fresco (Mexican fresh, soft cheese)
   or substitute Monterey Jack, sliced thinly
Slices of pickled jalapeño chiles
3 medium tomatoes, sliced thinly
3 cups finely shredded iceberg lettuce
PICKLED ONIONS (see recipe below)
CREAMY CHIPOTLE SAUCE (see recipe directly
above)

1. Marinate the chicken or turkey tenderloins in the mixture of olive oil, lemon or lime juice, garlic, salt and pepper for at least one hour. Broil or grill, turning the filets over once. Cook the chicken about ten minutes total per boned breast and the tenderloins about twenty-five minutes total. Set aside to cool and then slice them on the diagonal.

2. In order to assemble tortas, cut each bolillo in half and pull out some of the insides. Save for making future breadcrumbs. Smear one tablespoon of the Creamy Chipotle Sauce over each side of the roll. Press slices of cheese into the sauce. Next add three or four pickled onion rings. Add several slices of chicken or turkey slices, tomato slices, a little pile of shredded lettuce, and jalapeño slices. The torta should be stuffed to overflowing in order to be properly Mexican. Now press the two halves of the bolillo together and try to get your mouth around it.

PICKLED ONIONS FOR TORTAS

1 cup vinegar
1/2 cup water
1/2 teaspoon salt
1 tablespoon sugar
1 teaspoon crushed red peppers
1 teaspoon dried oregano
2 medium red onions, sliced thinly

1. Simmer everything but the onions together for five minutes. Pour the hot liquid over the onions slices and marinate for at least an hour before using. Store in refrigerator in glass jar to use in sandwiches and salads.

BARBECUE TORTA

A sandwich made with the best garlic bread.

6 to 8 bolillos
8 ounces butter or margarine
1/2 cup beer
2 cloves garlic, minced through a press
2 cups refried beans, warmed
1/4 cup lime juice
1 tablespoon olive oil

1 teaspoon garlic salt or Chipotle Spice Blend
 (see recipe on page 134)
2 pound flank steak, scored with knife
Creamy Chipotle Sauce (page 135)
2 avocados, sliced at last moment
3 cups thinly shredded romaine lettuce

1. Melt the butter and stir in the beer and minced garlic. Heat together to blend. Cut bolillos in half and pull out some of the crumbs (reserve for another use). Lavishly brush the insides of the bolillos with the garlic beer butter and set aside. Heat these over the barbecue grill or in oven at the very last moment before serving.

2. Heat the refried beans. You can use a good brand of canned beans or better still, your own homemade beans. I always make a big batch of beans and keep some in the freezer.

3. Marinate the flank steak in lime juice, olive oil, and seasoning for at one hour. Place the steak on a hot grill over coals covered with a white ash. Barbecue about twenty minutes. Let steak rest for fifteen minutes before slicing. Slice thinly across the grain. You can also broil the steak.

4. While the steak is resting before slicing, warm the bolillos over the grill or in the oven.

5. To assemble the tortas, spread about 1/4 cup refried beans over one-half of each warmed bolillo. Lay in about four slices of flank steak which should be drizzled with the Creamy Chipotle Sauce. Cover next with avocado slices and a pile of shredded romaine. Press on the top half bolillo. These are heavenly. You can pass more chipotle sauce or salsa at the table for those who never get enough fire.

Serves 6.

TINGA TORTA

Tinga is a spicy concoction from the city of Puebla, Mexico. It can be made with pork, chicken, or beef but it always contains chipotle chiles and chorizo sausage. It is so spicy it even warms the ear lobes.

As a plus, its flavors improve after a couple of days in the refrigerator, making it the perfect leftover. It can be served as a stew alongside rice or it is marvelous stuffed into a hollowed-out bolillo.

FIRST MAKE THE SAUCE:

*5 large, ripe tomatoes, broiled, skinned (about 2 and
   1/2 pounds) or 1 can plum tomatoes (28 oz.)*
3 cloves garlic
2 chipotle chiles adobado (from can)
2 teaspoons olive oil
2 medium onions, about 1 and 1/2 cups chopped
1/2 pound leanest, bulk Mexican chorizo sausage
2 tablespoons apple cider vinegar
2 tablespoons brown sugar
1/2 teaspoon salt
2 teaspoons adobo sauce from can
2 bay leaves
1/2 cinnamon stick
1/4 teaspoon cloves

THE MEAT:

1 tablespoon olive oil
2 pork tenderloins, about 1 pound each
2 cloves garlic, minced through a rpess
1/2 teaspoon salt
1/2 teaspoon freshly ground pepper
2 teaspoons dried oregano, crushed
2 bay leaves
1 onion, halved stuck with 4 cloves
1 and 1/2 cups water

142

GARNISH FOR TINGA

1 to 2 ripe avocados
1 red onion sliced into rings
3 chipotle chiles adobado, sliced for aficionados

1. Place tomatoes on a jelly roll pan about eight inches under a preheated broiler. Broil tomatoes until skins burst and are charred in places. This will take about ten minutes. Remove skins from tomatoes and half them horizontally. Hold each tomato half over the sink and squeeze out the seeds. Place tomatoes in bowl of food processor with garlic pieces and chipotle chiles. Chop into a coarse puree. If you are using canned tomatoes, place along with their juices in processor with rest of ingredients.

2. Heat a skillet with olive oil. Saute the onions for five minutes until softened. Remove and set aside. Using same skillet, fry the chorizo until well-cooked. Drain chorizo on paper towels while you wipe out the skillet. Return chorizo and onion to skillet and add the tomato-chipotle mixture along with vinegar, sugar, salt, adobo juice, spices and bay leaves. Simmer for twenty minutes to concentrate flavors. Reserve until you add the pork or chicken.

3. Dry pork tenderloins well with paper towels. Rub surfaces with minced garlic, salt, pepper, and oregano. Heat olive oil in a Dutch oven (I prefer using enameled cast-iron) and brown the meat very well. It should be entirely brown on all sides. Next add the bay leaves, onion, and water. Cover pot and place in a 350 degree oven for 1 and 1/2 hours. Check a couple of times to make sure there is liquid remaining in the pot. Add another 1/2 cup water if necessary. Remove the cooked meat from pot and cool for twenty minutes and then cut into slices. Pull meat into smaller pieces with your fingers.

4. Place shredded meat (in place of pork you may add cooked, shredded chicken) and tinga sauce into the Dutch oven with any remaining broth in pot. All the brown bits will add more flavor. Simmer for about twenty minutes. If the mixture seems dry, add 1/2 cup water or broth.

5. Serve the tinga garnished with avocado and red onion slices or stuff tinga into hollowed out bolillos. Smear the Creamy Chipotle Sauce (page 137) into the rolls. Add some shredded lettuce for crunch. Serves 6 to 8.

CHIPOTLE PORK CHOPS AND RISO

Someday I will clean out my outrageously over-stocked, messy pantry with all its mustards, vinegars, oils, six kinds of beans, four kinds of rice, and who knows how much pasta. One day I really needed just plain long grain rice rice and I couldn't locate it so I substituted riso, Italian rice-shaped pasta and what transpired was the birth of a recipe.

1 and 1/2 pounds well-trimmed loin pork chops
1 tablespoon olive oil
4 cloves garlic, minced
1 onion, chopped
1 red bell pepper, chopped
2 green chiles, charred, peeled, seeded, and chopped
1/2 pound chicken-cilantro sausage (see Note)
1 teaspoon olive oil
2 cups chicken broth (1 can reduced fat broth)
1/2 cup water
1 chipotle adobado plus1 tablespoon of sauce
1/2 teaspoon salt
1 and 1/2 cups riso
1/4 cups cilantro, snipped

1. Dry pork chops well and brown them in the olive oil using a heavy pot. I use an enameled cast-iron 6-

quart Dutch oven. After the chops are browned on both sides, remove them. Rub the teaspoon of olive oil over the sausages and cook until well-browned. Set aside. Using the same pot, saute the garlic, onion, bell pepper, and green chiles. This will take about eight minutes.

2. Mash the chipotle chile in a mortar or cut up finely with a chef's knife. Add the chipotle, the liquids, and salt to the pot of sauteed vegetables. Place the pork chops back into the pot. Simmer for fifteen minutes. Cut the sauages into slices.

3. Stir the riso and sausage in so they are immersed in the liquids and simmer for fifteen or twenty minutes until the liquid is absorbed. During the last five minutes, stir in one tablespoon of cilantro.

4. Sprinkle the rest of the cilantro over the tops of the pork chops and serve immediately. Serves 4 to 6.

Note: any sausage with a southwestern flavor will do in this recipe.

ROGER HAYOT'S CHILES WITH
SMOKED TOMATO SALSA

Roger's small but perfect little restaurant on Beverly Boulevard in Los Angeles sits on the same spot that his father's butcher shop did for forty years. He brings to his craft a knowledge of sausage making and spices that he got from the cradle. If we haven't visited the Authenic Cafe in a month, we start dreaming of Roger's Chile Rellenos, which are the best I have ever tasted, and his Chipotle Eggs over Cornbread. So we have to order both.

He very kindly shared his chile relleno recipe with me.

4 fresh poblano chiles
1 cup blue cornmeal
1 tablespoon cumin seeds, crushed
1/2 tablespoon dried granulated garlic
1 tablespoon freshly ground black pepper
1 tablespoon kosher salt
1/2 tablespoon crushed dried oregano
1/2 teaspoon cayenne pepper
2 cups grated Mozzarella cheese
1/2 cup grated smoked Mozzarella
1/4 cup grated Gouda cheese

1/2 cup minced cilantro
1/8 cup minced epazote (optional but good)
1/2 cup flour
3 eggs, beaten
2 cups canola oil for frying chiles

1. Char the chiles over a gas flame, grill, or small rack placed over a stove burner. Keep turning the chiles until they are fairly evenly blackened. Set aside to cool. Scrape off charred skin, then slit chiles down one side and cut out seed cores. Leave chiles as intact as possible.

2. Thoroughly blend the blue cornmeal, cumin seed, garlic, pepper, salt, oregano and cayenne pepper. Place mixture on a piece of waxed paper. Mix together the cheeses, cilantro and epazote if you are using it. Stuff equal amounts into each chile. Holding the stuffed chiles closed at the seams, roll gently in the flour, dip in beaten eggs, then coat in the spice and blue corn mixuture. Pat the spices onto the chiles until well-encrusted.

3. While you are preparing the chiles, you can have the oil heating in a deep pan (like cast-iron) over medium heat. Fry the chiles, spooning hot oil over them until they turn a rich golden brown. Drain on paper towels. Serve with Roger's Tomato-Chipotle Salsa. Serves 4.

*Per serving (without sauce): 480 calories, 28 g pro-
tein, 31 g carbohydrate, 27 g fat (10 g saturated), 151
mg cholesterol, 1,273 mg sodium, 3 g fiber.*

Nutritional note: if you wish to cut down on fat con-
tent you could use a low-fat Mozzarella cheese for
the filling and a smaller amount per chile, such as 1/2
cup. You could also lower the salt to just 1/2 teaspoon
for the coating.

SMOKED TOMATO-CHIPOTLE SALSA

*10 medium tomatoes
1 onion
1 tablespoon minced garlic
1 tablespoon canned chipotle chile adobado
1/2 teaspoon freshly ground pepper
Juice of 1 lime
3/4 tablespoon kosher salt*

1. Grill the tomatoes and onion over a wood fire or
under the gas flame of a broiler until lightly charred.
Peel onion, quarter and put in a food processor along
with the grilled tomatoes which you have also peeled.
A few charred bits of skin are okay as they just add
character to the sauce. Chop in pulses so the sauce is
of a medium puree with some texture. Add the garlic,
chipotle, pepper, lime juice, and salt. Pulsate again to
blend.

Serve about 1/2 cup salsa per chile relleno. People love to dip tortillas into it. Makes about 1 quart.

Per 1/2 serving: 43 calories, 2 g protein, 10 g carbohydrate, 0 fat, 0 cholesterol, 628 mg sodium, 3 g fiber.

CALDO DE TLALPEÑO

According to an old Western tale the granddaughter of Kit Carson fondly remembered a version of this soup from her childhood. Perhaps Kit Carson himself dined on Caldo de Tlalpeño along the Camino Real and brought the recipe home. The distinctive flavor of the soup is due to the chipotles adobados. Caldo tlalpeño qualifies as a Mexican dry soup for there is very little broth in relationship to the long line of enticing ingredients.

1 and 1/2 quarts caldo (chicken broth)
1 whole chicken breast, skin removed
3 small tomatoes, broiled, skins removed
1 small onion, about 1/2 cup, in quarters
3 cloves garlic, minced
2 chipotle chiles adobado (from can)
2 teaspoons adobado sauce
1 teaspoon dried oregano
*2 leaves fresh epazote or 1 teaspoon dried epazote
  (optional)*

150

2 to 3 teaspoons olive oil for sauteeing
1 and 1/2 cups cooked garbanzo beans,
   low sodium or use home-cooked
1 bunch carrots, peeled, 2-inch pieces
3 cups cooked brown rice (see Note)
1/2 cup minced green onions, including some of tops
1 and 1/2 cups cubed Monterey Jack cheese
1 avocado, peeled and diced

1. Bring the chicken broth to a simmer and add the
breast, cooking it just until done or about twenty
minutes.

2. Meanwhile, broil the tomatoes or hold them over a
flame just until they are blackened around the edges.
Remove the skins and cut tomatoes into pieces. Place
in the bowl of a food processor along with the onion
quarters, garlic, oregano, epazote, chipotles and adobo
sauce. Chop into a coarse puree. (If you had any of
Roger's Smoked Tomato Chipotle Salsa, you could
substitute 1 and 1/2 cups Salsa for this step).

3. Saute the tomato-chipotle puree in the olive oil for
five minutes to concentrate the flavors.

4. Remove the chicken breast from the broth and set
aside to cool. Stir the tomato-chipotle puree into the
chicken broth. Simmer together for twenty minutes.

Add the carrots. Simmer for ten minutes. Dice the chicken breast and add to the simmering broth along with the garbanzos. The soup is now ready to be served.

5. You can line up little dishes of the accompaniments: hot rice, minced green onions, cheese cubes,and avocado cubes for your guests to add to their own bowls or you can do it in the kitchen. Spoon about 1/3 cup hot rice into wide, shallow soup bowls. Next add 1/4 cup cheese cubes and ladle in a cup of soup. Sprinkle the avocado cubes and green onions over the tops and serve. Serves 6.

Note: to steam brown rice, stir one cup rice into 2 1/2 cups boiling water. Add 1 teaspoon salt and 2 teaspoons butter. Steam rice for about 40 minutes.

SMOKED CHICKEN TAMALES WITH SMOKY CORN SALSA

This is an adaptation of a recipe by Michele Anna Jordan, owner of the Jaded Palate Catering Company in Sonoma, California. At first, I hesitated at using Michele's idea of chipotle puree in the tamale dough, the filling, and the salsa. I thought it would be overpowering but the chipotle fires up every layer of taste in the tamale and results in some of the best tamales I have ever tasted. The only way I change the recipe is to add canola oil in place of some of the lard and to add more ingredients to the filling. We love the Nicaraguan nacatamales which have a greater variety of ingredients in their fillings as opposed to typical Mexican tamales. Hint: before you begin this recipe, puree a whole seven-ounce can of chipotles adobados. Remove the chile stems and some of the seeds and puree the chipotles along with the adobo juices in a food processor. Use the puree for this recipe and reserve the rest in a glass jar. You can use the rest of the puree in salsas, in more tamales, or for the Sonoran Enchiladas given in the next recipe.

TAMALE DOUGH

1 package of dried corn husks (hojas)
2 cups masa harina (dehydrated masa) Quaker brand
1 teaspoon baking powder
1 teaspoon salt
1/3 cup lard
1/2 cup canola oil
1 and 1/2 tablespoons pureed canned chipotle chiles
1 and 1/2 cups hot chicken broth

FILLING

1 tablespoon canola oil
1 medium onion, about 3/4 cup diced
4 cloves garlic, minced
1 and 1/2 cups smoked chicken, coarsely chopped
2 tablespoons pureed, canned chipotle chiles
1/4 cup chicken broth
3 teaspoons capers
1/2 cup sliced black olives
1/3 cup raisins, plumped in hot water or in microwave
1 cooked Russet potato, about 1 and 1/2 cups diced

CHIPOTLE CORN SALSA:

2 ears of very fresh corn
2 ripe tomatoes
1 small red onion (3/4 cup)
2 jalapeño chiles, cored, minced
3/4 cup chopped red bell pepper
2 teaspoons pureed, canned chipotle chiles
Juice of 2 limes
1 tablespoon olive oil
1/4 cup cilantro, snipped

1. Soak the corn husks for at least one hour before you will need them. A sinkful of hot water works best for soaking. To prepare the tamale dough, place the dry ingredients in the bowl of a heavy-duty mixer (like Kitchen-Aid). To this, add the small amount of lard (used just for flavor) and blend it into the masa harina using the paddle attachment. Slowly add the canola oil while the mixer is blending. Next add the pureed chipotles and the hot broth. Beat the dough about two minutes or until it makes a slapping noise against the bowl of the mixer. If the dough does not make a slapping noise, you need to add more hot broth. Add one tablespoon at a time. You cannot have runny dough or it will not adhere to the husks. Set dough aside while you make the filling.

2. Saute the onion until softened. Add the garlic during the last minute. Stir in the smoked chicken, pureed chipotles, the chicken broth, capers, olives, and raisins. Simmer for a couple of minutes just to blend flavors. At the last minute, stir in the diced potatoes and cilantro. Salt to taste. This is a very delicious filling that could also be used to make glamorous soft tacos. All you need is some crunchy romaine and salsa.

3. To assemble the tamales: remove the corn husks from the hot water and drain on paper towels, blotting excess moisture. Pick out the largest husks for the tamales. Tear the narrower husks into strips to be used for tying the tamales. Spread about 1/4 cup masa mixture inside the rounded portion of the husk. Spread masa up to one-inch from sides of husk. Leave bare at least two-inches on each end to allow for tying up the tamale. Place a generous two table-spoons of filling mostly in the center of the husk. You may use more filling if you happen to have a large husk. Roll the tamale up and tie each end with a strip of husk or a piece of cotton string. Continue making the rest of the tamales. This recipe will make about twelve big tamales.

4. I use a multi-layered aluminum Chinese steamer. A large vegetable steamer or a traditional tamale pot works also. Bring two-inches of water to boil under the steamer rack. Lay the tamales on the rack. It's okay if you have to lay some on top of others. With a Chinese steamer, you can place the tamales in two levels so they are not crowded. Steam the tamales for fifty minutes. The dough should pull away easily from the husk when they are done. If you make small tamales, they may be done in only forty minutes. While the tamales are steaming you can make the corn

salsa or you can make the salsa the night before as it gains wonderful flavor as it sits.

5. To make the corn salsa: remove the husks and silk from the corn. Rinse. Simmer in rapidly boiling water for two minutes. Cool down in a bowl of cold water. Cut off the kernels from the cobs. Cut all the tomatoes, onions, and red pepper into about the same size dice. When you core the jalapeños, save some of the seeds to add to the salsa. Mince the chiles and add to above mixture. Stir in the pureed chipotles, lime juice, olive oil, cilantro, and salt. Serve this salsa alongside the tamales. Makes about 3 cups salsa.

The tamales will feed about 6 hearty eaters.

SONORAN ENCHILADAS

This recipe, an adaptation from James Peyton's excellent El Norte, The Cuisine of Northern Mexico, captivated my club of taste testers because they had never tasted chipotles used in enchiladas and they all asked for second helpings. I loved his accompanying story of spending the night at a remote Mexican rancho where the cook provided these enchiladas and carne asada for dinner.

2 and 1/2 tablespoons butter
2 and 1/2 tablespoons flour
1 cup of Campbell's beef broth
1 cup water
2 tablespoons chipotle puree (see above tamale recipe)
3 garlic cloves, minced
1 and 1/2 teaspoons oregano
1 teaspoon toasted cumin seed, crushed in mortar
1/4 cup light sour cream (reduced fat)
12 thin, very fresh corn tortillas
1 cup minced onion,
   reserve 1/4 cup for topping)
12 ounces sharp Cheddar or Chihuahua cheese, grated
   (reserve 1/2 cup for topping)
1/4 cup canola oil for frying tortillas

1. Grind the toasted cumin seeds in a mortar or a spice grinder. Add the garlic and oregano and mash into a paste.

2. Melt the butter in a skillet and stir in the flour.

Cook the roux over medium heat until it is a light brown. Remove pan from heat and slowly whisk in the broth. Place back over medium heat and continue to whisk as you add the water. Add the cumin-garlic-oregano paste along with the chipotle puree. Simmer the sauce uncovered for about twenty minutes. The sauce will reduce and thicken. Remove the pan from the heat and whisk in the sour cream. Set aside.

3. Have your minced onions and grated cheese ready for your enchilada assembly line so as you soften the tortillas your fillings will be ready to use. Grease two baking dishes (approximately nine by twelve inches) and have them ready for the filled enchiladas.

4. Heat a couple of teaspoons of oil in a ten-inch nonstick skillet. Soften two tortillas at a time in the hot oil. Turn the tortillas with tongs and fry the other side just until they are softened and puffy. Lay the tortillas out on a flat plate and quickly place a heaping tablespoon of cheese toward one edge and a table-spoon of minced onion. Roll the enchiladas up into cylinders. Place in baking dish.

5. Adding more oil to the skillet, keep softening two tortillas at a time and then filling the enchiladas. I have tried to entirely eliminate this frying step but it serves to seal the tortillas and keeps them from falling apart when they are used for enchiladas.

6. Once you have rolled up all the enchiladas, cover them well with the chipotle sauce. Sprinkle the tops with the reserved chopped onion and grated cheese. Bake briefly in a preheated 375 degree oven for no more than 8 to 10 minutes or just until the sauce is bubbling. Serve with rice, beans, and barbecued chicken or steak.

Serves 6.

MEATBALLS IN CHIPOTLE SAUCE

These meatballs have gone to tailgate picnics in an elegant copper chafing dish. They are spooned into crusty Italian rolls and adored by all.

CHIPOTLE SAUCE:

1 tablespoon oil
1/2 onion, chopped
1 clove garlic, minced
1 can crushed tomatoes (28 ounces) with added puree
1 and 1/2 cups reduced-fat chicken broth
2 chipotle chiles adovado from can, finely minced or
 use 2 tablespoons chipotle puree

MEATBALLS:

1 pound ground round steak (15 % fat)
1 pound ground turkey or pork
1 slice bread, crust removed
1/2 cup milk
4 green onions, minced
1/4 cup minced white onion
1/4 cup minced parsley
1 egg
1 teaspoon salt
1 teaspoon oregano
1/2 teaspoon freshly ground pepper
1/4 teaspoon freshly ground nutmeg
1/4 teaspoon cinnamon

1. Saute the onion in the oil until softened and then add the garlic, crushed tomatoes, broth, and chipotle chiles. Simmer the sauce for about twenty minutes while you prepare the meatballs.

2. Soak the bread in the milk just until absorbed and then squeeze out the milk. Crumble the bread into the ground meats. Next stir in the green onions, onion, parsley, egg, salt, oregano, pepper, nutmeg, and cinnamon. Blend with a large spoon or work it all together with your hands.

3. Preheat oven to 400 degrees. Form the meatballs

about the size of golfballs and place in a roasting pan. Bake for twenty-five minutes or until lightly browned.

4. Add the browned meatballs to the pot containing the chipotle sauce. Simmer for at least fifteen minutes. Serve immediately or cool them in the sauce. They reheat beautifully in a chafing dish if you are going to carry them to a tailgate picnic or a buffet.

Serves 6 if placed inside Italian or French rolls

HONEY CHIPOTLE BARBECUE SAUCE

This is good drizzled over barbecued chicken, slices of flank steak, chicken or turkey cutlets, or pork loin. The fire of the chipotle blends perfectly with the sweet ingredients. You won't be sorry when you try this one.

4 chipotle chiles adobados from can, stems removed
3 cloves garlic
1/4 cup honey
2 tablespoons brown sugar
2 tablespoons Dijon mustard with seeds
1/4 cup apple cider vinegar
1/2 teaspoon cumin seed, crushed
2 tablespoons cilantro
1/2 teaspoon salt

1. Place all the ingredients in the bowl of a food processor and puree into a sauce consistency. Makes about 2/3 cup sauce.

SALSA DE CHIPOTLE

While staying in Oaxaca, Mexico last summer, we enjoyed this salsa in several restaurants including our favorite one, Mi Casita. The heat level varied but the one constant was the chipotle chile, a favorite in Oaxaca.

2 dried chiles chipotles
2 dried chiles anchos or pasillas
2 medium ripe tomatoes
6 tomatillos (the green-husked Mexican tomatoes)
1/4 cup red or white chopped onion
2 cloves garlic, minced
1/4 cup water
1/2 teaspoon salt
1/4 cup cilantro

1. Toast the chiles on a griddle until softened. Soak in hot water for one hour. Place chiles in a food processor with 1/4 cup fresh water and puree.

2. Grill or broil tomatoes just until the skin loosens and is slightly charred. Remove skins and cores from tomatoes. Rinse the tomatillos in warm water and

remove husks. Grill or broil them just until they are softened.

3. Place the chile puree, tomatoes, tomatillos, onion, garlic, salt, and cilantro into processor and roughly puree into a salsa with texture. Makes about 2 and 1/3 cups salsa. Serve with eggs, fish, or chicken.

QUESADILLAS WITH SMOKED FIRE SALSA

"You will never starve if you can make good omelets and quesadillas", is the advice I have frequently re- peated to my sons. Quesadillas, using flour tortillas, were the first snacks they learned to cook.
The tortillas should be fresh so they don't crack when you fold them over. Just a couple of tablespoons of sharp Cheddar or Monterey Jack are needed in the middle. Toast the quesadilla in a hot dry skillet until the cheese melts and the tortilla turns a bit golden around the edges. Serve with salsa such as Smoked Fire.

1 can plum tomatoes (28 ounces), drained
3 to 6 chipotle chiles adobados from can
2 teaspoons adobo juice from can
1 tablespoon olive oil
2 teaspoons lime juice
3 cloves garlic

1. Place all of the ingredients in a food processor and puree. Only use the larger amount of chipotles if you have an incredible tolerance for heat. Remember that the chipotle type of fire is cumulative.

2. Simmer the salsa for five minutes in a saucepan just to concentrate the flavors. This salsa is also good when spread out over an entire flour tortilla and then sprinkled with grated cheese. Broil until bubbly for an open-faced quesadilla. Makes about 2 cups salsa.

LOW -FAT TURKEY CHILI WITH CHIPOTLE

This chili is packed with a myriad of flavors that bombard your palate and you don't have to feel guilty about eating it because one serving only has 6 grams of fat.

12 ounces beer, do not use dark beer
2 cups chopped onion
3/4 cup chopped red bell pepper
1 and 1/2 tablespoons minced garlic
3 bay leaves
1 tablespoon dried oregano
1 tablespoon crushed cumin seeds
1 pound ground turkey
1/2 teaspoon salt
1/4 teaspoon freshly ground pepper

2 jalapeño chiles, veins and seeds removed, sliced
2 (18 and 3/4 ounces each) cans natural whole
  tomatoes with juice
1/4 cup New Mexican chile powder (Dixon is perfect)
1 dried chipotle chile, ground into coarse powder
1 and 1/2 pounds turkey tenderloins (about 2)
3 cups cooked pinto or black beans
  or 2 cans black beans (15 ounces each), drained
2 tablespoons Quaker masa harina
1/2 cup water
1/4 cup cilantro, snipped

1. Using an eight-quart heavy pot, simmer the onion, bell pepper, garlic, bay leaves, oregano, and cumin in the beer until it is almost reduced by half. This step takes the place of sauteeing the ingredients in oil as you are literally sauteeing in beer. To this mixture, add the ground turkey and simmer for another ten minutes. Break up the turkey using a large spoon. There should be no large chunks. Sprinkle meat with salt and pepper. Next add the jalapeño slices.

2. Roughly puree the tomatoes and their juices in a food processor. Add to the ground turkey. Stir in the chile powder and chipotle powder. Bring to a gentle simmer.

3. Cut the turkey tenderloins into one-half inch thick

slices and roughly dice. Add diced turkey to the chili
brewing in the pot. Simmer for thirty minutes. The
raw turkey will release its juices into the chili as it
simmers adding great flavor. Stir in the beans and
simmer for ten more minutes.

4. If your chili needs thickening, stir the masa harina
into the water to make a smooth paste. Blend half of
the paste into the pot, stirring well. If your chili still
needs more thickening, stir in the rest of the masa
paste. Simmer for a few more minutes. Sprinkle in
the cilantro.

For an attractive presentation to guests, the chili can
be served with bowls of condiments such as sliced
avocado, olives, chopped red onion, minced cilantro,
and grated cheese.

Serves 8 medium bowls.

*Per serving: calories: 340; protein: 39 g; carbohy-
drates: 29 g; fat: 6 g; cholesterol: 91 g; sodium:
446 g; fiber: 10 g.*

CHAPTER VI

BREADS TO GO WITH CHILES
AND CHILE BREADS

If you love something, whether it be garlic,
chocolate or chiles, it is easy enough to go
overboard and put IT in everything. I have
tried to control myself in the chile department
although my sons are beginning to wonder if
they will ever again see the sunny side of a
roast beef. If you are having a simple dinner of

grilled steak or chicken, chile breads or jalapeño corn muffins are a good addition. However, to serve chile breads with picante enchildas or pots of chile is simply feeding the fire with flames. These days, jalapeños are even finding their way into bagels, but the palate needs relief so I have included here the breads like sopaipillas and my traditional flour tortillas which serve as a perfect foil for spicy meals. If you eat something too hot, the best medicine is bread (chased down by chocolate).

SOPAIPILLAS

In the Southwest, sopaipillas are served in great quantities as part of the meal and usually never as a dessert although they resemble the puffy palillas that we served dusted with powdered sugar for breakfast and holidays on our rancho. This recipe is in my *California Rancho Cooking*. The proper way to eat a sopaipilla is to bit off a small corner and drizzle in golden honey.

If you're not careful, you could eat a basket of sopaipillas before you know it. They are a welcome relief when you are dining on hot New Mexican chile so I hope no one comes along and puts jalapeños in them.

3 and 3/4 cups all-purpose flour
1 and 1/2 tespoons salt
1 and 1/2 teapoons baking powder
3 tablespoons shortening (Crisco)
1 teaspoon dry yeast (1/3 of a package)
3 tablespoons warm water
Pinch of sugar
1 cup evaporated milk plus 2 tablespoons,
    warmed to 108 degrees
2 cups light oil for frying

1.   Stir together flour, salt, and baking powder in bowl. Using a fork or pastry blender, mix in the shortening until blended evenly throughout the dry ingredients.

2. Dissolve the yeast and sugar in warm water. Let it sit about five minutes. Add it to the warm milk and slowly stir into the flour, drizzling it throughout the mixture. Knead the dough right in the bowl, adding up to two tablespoons of

water if the mixture seems dry. Knead it for one minute or just long enough to form into a cohesive ball.

3. Cover with plastic wrap and let it rest for 30 minutes.

4. Punch down the dough and divide it in half. Wrap the half that you will not be using right away so it does not dry out.

5. Roll out the dough half into a rectangle, less than one-fourth inch thickness. Fold the dough in half and roll out again. If the edges are uneven, trim them off with a pastry wheel or sharp knife and discard. Uneven edges with a varying thickness will cause problems in puffing the sopaipillas. Cut into 12 rectangles.

6. Heat the oil in a deep saucepan (I use a two-quart pan) to about 360 degrees. Line a jelly roll pan with several thicknesses of paper towels. Drop in one square of dough. It will first sink and then rise to the surface. Immediately spoon hot oil over the top continuously and the sopaipilla will keep puffing. Many recipes will tell you to hold the sopaipilla under the oil but

172

this is not as effective as the spooning technique in insuring puffing. When the sopaipilla is a deep golden brown on the bottom side turn it over to brown the other side. Lift it out and place on paper towels. Blot the top. Add the next piece of dough to the oil. You will have to work quickly now.

7. Turn off the oil for the two minutes it will take you to roll out the other half of the dough. Turn the oil back on just as you are cutting out the rectangles. Fry the rest of the sopaipillas and drain. Eat immediately if you don't already have a growing audience accumulating around the kitchen. Sopaipillas are best right out of the pan and hold well for as long as a half an hour to forty five minutes. Most New Mexican restaurants only cook them to order. This recipe makes about 25 sopaipillas. If you do not want to cook them all at once, you can store half of the dough, well-wrapped in plastic, in the refrigerator overnight. Serve sopaipillas during the meal or for breakfast. They are wonderful with apricot jam drizzled inside and a cup of strong coffee.

BLUE CORN MADELEINES

Blue corn has definitely made an inroad into the popular food consciousness of today but to the Pueblo Indians of the Southwest, it is a staple. Blue Squaw corn is grown commercially near San Juan Pueblo in New Mexico. The corn itself is almost a purplish color and it has an earthier, more corny flavor than white or yellow corn. Blue corn comes in many guises. It can be a fine, toasted flour for atole, a coarse grind for breads, or lime-treated harinilla for blue corn tortillas. The toasted flour, whether fine or coarse, lends a delicacy to breads and muffins It is available in many gourmet stores and health food stores or you can send for it. See Resources at back of book.

This particular recipe for muffins baked in madeleine tins was inspired by the Salisbury family's Sonora Cafe in downtown Los Angeles where the food is elegant Southwestern and they are kind enough to keep basketfuls of these muffins for people that can't stop eating when they should!

174

1 cup all-purpose flour
1 cup blue corn flour
1/4 cup sugar
1 tablespoon baking powder
1/2 teaspoon baking soda
1 teaspoon salt
1 egg
1/4 cup melted butter
1 and 1/2 cups buttermilk

1. You will need at least two madeleine plaques but it is alright to bake in two batches. Muffin tins can be used also as this recipe makes about 12 regular muffins or about 24 madeleine muffins. Spray the indentations with baker's spray or rub with soft butter.

2. Sift together dry ingredients. Beat the egg and then add the cooled, melted butter, and buttermilk. Pour over the dry ingredients, blending well so that no dry spots remain but do not overmix.

3. Spoon batter into the tins, filling each de-
pression about three-quarters full. Bake at 425
degrees for 15 minutes or bake muffins for 20
minutes. Serve with spicy meals accompanied
by butter or honey butter: blend one-half cup
of softened butter or margarine with four to six
tablespoons of honey.

TRADITIONAL FLOUR TORTILLAS

Traditional flour tortillas, as they were done on
the ranchos of California, were a custom
brought up from northern Mexico by the mi-
grating Spanish settlers. In Sonora, they pride
themselves on being able to stretch a tortilla the
length of an arm but on our California rancho,
the delicacy and thinness of your tortilla was as
important as size. When these homemade,
handstretched tortillas are brushed with butter,
sprinkled with cinnamon and sugar, and baked
in a hot oven until crisp, they are like layered
pastry. They are also wonderful to use for
California Tortilla Pizza.

176

Tips for the Perfect Tortilla

1. Use warm water for mixing. Hot water makes the flour granules swell, causing a chewier tortilla.

2. Allow for both recommended resting periods. The dough will be much easier to handle. The resting is very important since it will make the difference between a rough dough and smooth, relaxed dough.

3. Place the resting dough in a warm place but not in the oven.

4. When rolling out each tortilla, do not use too much flour. The tortilla needs to get a grip on the board.

5. Before rolling your first tortilla, preheat heavy, ungreased griddle preferably of rolled steel or cast-iron. When the griddle is ready, a couple of drops of water will bounce.

6. Do not use a spatula to turn tortillas. Push your thumb into the edge of the tortilla, grab and turn in one swift action of the hand.

7. The most efficient rolling pin for flour tortillas is the palo used by the grande dames of tortilla making. It is a seven-inch dowel or sawed-off broom handle. Sand and clean before using.

4 cups unbleached, all-purpose flour
Pinch of baking powder (1/8 teaspoon)
2 very rounded tablespoons vegetable
   shortening (1/3 cup)
 About 1 and 1/2 cups warm water
1 and 1/2 teaspoons salt

1. Dissolve the salt in the warm water and set aside. Using a pastry blender or large fork, work the shortening into the flour and baking powder until it is mealy and there are no powdery remains of flour. Use your fingertips to finish working the fat into the flour.

2. While you are lifting up the flour with the fork, slowly add the warm water. Drizzle the water into different parts of the bowl. When you have added all but a tablespoon of water, start pushing the dough together. If you feel a

178

dry spot, drizzle in the tablespoon of water. If
the dough does not form a soft ball, not too
sticky, add water by the teaspoonful but usually
one and a half cups of water are adequate. Dust
the dough lightly with flour and knead for no
more than one minute. If you like tough, rub-
bery tortillas (which some people do) then
knead the dough for at least 10 minutes.

3.   Wrap dough in plastic wrap or leave on
floured board covered with the upside down
mixing bowl. ALLOW THE DOUGH TO
REST FOR AT LEAST 45 MINUTES.   Make
sure it does not dry out on the surface.

4.   After the resting period, pinch off 12 to 15
pieces of dough and form into balls. Rotate the
ball in one hand as you smooth the edges
underneath Place each ball of dough on a
greased baking sheet and, using the heel of your
hand, flatten each ball. While you are working
keep the pieces of dough well covered with
plastic wrap. Allow the dough to rest from 45
minutes to one hour. You may refrigerate the
dough from two hours to one day at this point.
Let the dough warm up for at least one-half
hour before you try to roll out tortillas.

5. When you are ready to roll tortillas, preheat your griddle over medium heat. Lightly dust your board with flour and place flattened ball of dough in center, keeping the rest of the dough well-covered so it does not dry out. Begin rolling the dough into a thick circle. Using short, quick strokes, roll from the center to the edge of the circle. Make a quarter turn of the tortilla after each two short strokes and your tortilla will remain round. By frequently lifting up the tortilla and making a quarter turn before rolling, it is easier to them round instead of violin-shaped. Violins still taste good.

6.   After you have rolled an eight-inch circle, you may *handstretch* your tortilla to a thin ten-inch circle. Hang the tortilla on the fingertips of one hand while you draw the fingertips of the other hand across the bottom of the tortilla, pulling and stretching gently toward you. Perform this stretching twice in each direction to make the tortilla round and amazingly thin. You cannot achieve this with just rolling. Enchiladas made with these tortillas will be light and puffy as though you had used crepes.

7.   Cook the tortilla on the hot griddle. Keep turning it over every ten seconds for about a minute. After you turn it over the first time, it will puff in spots, sometimes dramatically, and begin to develop golden spots. Do not push on the tortilla where it is puffing as it is forming layers. This is the difference between your tortilla and the store-bought kind. When you have turned the tortilla over four or five times and it is not puffing any longer, it is done.

Put your finished tortillas in a piece of foil or wrap in a clean dish towel. If well-wrapped in a plastic bag, they will keep in the refrigerator for a week. Freshen up tortillas by placing them on a hot griddle and turning until warm and soft again

This recipe produces from twelve to fifteen flour tortillas depending upon whether or not you have been cooking and eating very many.

Care of your tortilla griddle: Before conditioning a new griddle (whether cast-iron or rolled steel), wash off residue with hot water and soap. If you want the griddle to develop an antique blackened look then rub it on the top with vegetable oil. Place it directly on medium heat for one-half hour. The steel will darken with tempering. To clean a tortilla griddle, scrape off remains of dough or flour with a spatula, rinse the griddle under hot water, and dry with paper towels.

JALAPEÑO AND CHILE FLAVORED TORTILLAS
AND FLOUR TORTILLA CHIPS

The only time I flavor tortillas is when I am serving them as an appetizer or with a simple grilled chicken or steak. I have tried mincing up canned jalapeños (the fresh ones are too crisp) and mixing them into my tortilla dough but even tiny bits of chile tend to tear the dough during the stretching step. It is much more easy to make flavored butters and brush them onto the flour tortillas as they are being toasted in the oven or grilled.

182

6 10-inch flour tortillas
1/2 cup melted butter
1 or 2 fresh or canned jalapeño chiles, seeded,
  stemmed, minced or 2 teaspoons mild ground
  chile

1. Stir either the minced chiles (add two if you like it hot) or the ground chile into the melted butter.

2. If you want to serve triangles of flavored flour tortilla chips for an appetizer with drinks, just stack up two tortillas on top of one another and cut into eight triangles. Lay out the triangles on two baking sheets and brush just the tops with the flavored butters. If you do both flavors, alternating the green jalapeño and the red chile chips on a platter, they make a beautiful presentation. Toast in a preheated 375 oven degrees for about 18 minutes to 20 minutes or until crisp and golden. If you want the flavors to be more intense, brush the chips again after they have been in the oven for 10 minutes.

3. If you just want to flavor your tortillas rather than make tortilla chips, you may brush the flavored butter on the tortillas and warm them in a preheated 375 degree oven for five minutes.

BOB'S GRILLED TORTILLAS

My husband Bob does not cook but every five years he is struck by such a flash of creativity in the kitchen that it even amazes him. He is one of my most discriminating tasters and although he may not know why something is right or wrong, he instinctively knows. He just knows. One night when we were grilling chicken filets with a lime-garlic marinade, he came in with a few flour tortillas that he had brushed with the same marinade and then grilled also. They were astoundingly good and I wondered why we had never thought of it before.

Flour tortillas, about 6
Juice of 2 limes
1 or 2 cloves of garlic, minced through press
2 tablespoons olive oil

1. Mix the marinade together. Brush on one side of the flour tortillas and place on barbecue grill about six inches over whitened coals. Do this just as you are almost finished grilling your meat. You want the tortillas to actually grill and get a little toasty on the bottom sides. This

184

is enough marinade for about six 10-inch flour tortillas. Bob did not saturate them but just brushed them lightly with the lime mixture.

CALIFORNIA TORTILLA PIZZA

In Arizona, they make something wonderful called Cheese Crisps which are deep-fried flour tortillas finished off with lots of melted cheese and chile strips. I have found an easier system of crisping tortillas by placing them on dark, heavy baking sheets and brushing with melted butter. If the oven is good and hot, the flour tortilla will become crisp and golden.

4 large flour tortillas (one per person)
1/4 cup melted butter
1 cup green or red salsa, page 117 and 120
2 cups shredded Jack or Italian Fontina
4 large green chiles, cut into thin strips
  (canned is O.K)
4 jalapeños en escabeche, canned, cut
  into rings

1. Preheat the oven to 400 degrees. Place the flour tortillas on two baking sheets. Brush

lightly with butter on one side. Place in oven for eight to ten minutes to BEGIN the crisping of the tortillas.

2. Remove the baking sheets from oven and brush the tortillas lightly with salsa. Sprinkle with cheese. Lay eight thin strips of chile on each tortilla in a pinwheel design. Place jalapeño rings between each strip.

3. Put baking sheets back in hot oven for another eight to ten minutes or until pizzas are golden and bubbly. To serve, cut into triangles with a pizza wheel. Serve with salad for a whole meal or serve as an appetizer. Plan about one tortilla per person.

JALAPEÑO ROLLS

These rolls are what you need to accompany a plain dinner of roasted or grilled meat or fish. You can make them into long French roll shapes, brush them with an egg white wash and they will make superb sandwiches or you can

make them into round, fat shapes and use them
for the best grilled hamburgers you've ever had.

1 package dry yeast
1 teaspoon sugar
1/4 cup warm water (108 degrees)
3/4 cup warm milk (108 degrees)
2 whole eggs
1 teaspoon salt
2 tablespoons sugar
3 or 4 fresh jalapeño chiles, seeded, stemmed,
  minced
3 and 3/4 cups flour
1 and 1/4 cups grated sharp Cheddar cheese
1/4 cup finely grated Parmesan cheese

1. Mix yeast and sugar in the warm wate and
proof until puffy.

2. In a large mixing bowl, place the warm milk,
eggs, salt, sugar, chiles, and yeast mixture.
Beat in one cup of flour until well blended.
Next add the grated cheeses and slowly add
flour by one-half cups at at time. You may not
need all of the flour so hold back at least on
one-half cup for kneading.

3. Place the dough on a floured board and knead for eight minutes.

4. Place the dough in a greased bowl covered with plastic wrap. Let rise until double, about one hour.

5. Form the dough into 18 balls, shaping them into rounds by turning the edges under toward the center of the ball. Brush them with an egg wash (one egg white plus one tablespoon water) if you want them to be crusty. You may also form them into hamburger bun shapes or French roll shapes.

6. Let them rise about 30 minutes or until double. Bake in a preheated 375 degree oven for 12 to 15 minutes.

GREEN CHILE FRENCH LOAVES

These are a delicious sacrilege. I turned my favorite French baguettes that I used to savor with sweet butter and strawberry jam into Green Chile Loaves and I'm not even sorry.

188

1/2 cup warm water (108 degrees)
3 teaspoons dry yeast
1 tablespoon sugar
2 cups warm water
3 teaspoons salt
6 cups of unbleached bread flour (high protein)
1/2 cup flour for kneading
1 can green chiles (7 oz.), rinsed and patted dry, chopped
5 fresh jalapeño chiles, seeded, stemmed, minced
7 ounces mozzarella cheese, sliced thinly

1. Proof yeast in the water and sugar for 10 minutes until puffy.

2. In a large mixing bowl, place the two cups warm water, the salt, and the yeast mixture. Add two cups flour to the liquid and beat with a large wooden spoon or a whisk to aerate the dough. Next add flour slowly.

3. When the dough is stiff, place it on a floured board and knead, adding flour by the tablespoon as needed. Knead for 10 minutes.

4. Allow the dough to rise for one hour or until

doubled. Punch down and divide the dough into four pieces. Use your hands to roll each piece into a 10-inch thick rope. Place on a greased baking sheet. Cut a slit down the center of the rope to within one- half inch of the bottom. Sprinkle a mixture of the green chiles and jalapeño chiles down the center, pressing them into the dough. Cover the chiles with slices of cheese.

5. Let the loaves rise for about 20 minutes or until almost doubled. Bake in a preheated 375 degree oven for 35 minutes or until loaves are golden brown. Makes four loaves.

This dough makes excellent baguettes so you really could leave one loaf plain for your bread and jam in the morning. I serve the Green Chile French Loaves for picnics or to accompany barbecued steaks. They are best the day they are baked. If you anticipate having any leftover, wrap the loaf tightly in foil and freeze. To thaw, bake at 350 degrees for about 25 minutes and it will be as good as the day you baked it.

PIZZA BREAD WITH CHIPOTLE CHILES

This is a recipe my mother often baked as learned from an Italian neighbor who thought pizza should be about 2-inches thick or it was not pizza. In those days, it was always covered with a layer of sauteed onions and then a layer of homemade tomato sauce. No cheese. My mother baked it in a long jelly roll pan and it seldom lasted more than the time it took to be cool enough to eat. I have also baked it just rubbed with virgin olive oil and fresh garlic.

Every summer when we sail to Santa Cruz Island, THE PIZZA is baked in my little alcohol-fueled boat oven. To perpetuate this well-loved recipe into my chile era, I took inspiration from Edward Espe Brown of Tassajara reknown and author of many superb books, who recommends rubbing pizza with chipotle puree. I have added fresh minced garlic and olive oil to canned chipotles en adobo for the rub, giving the pizza a hot, smoky flavor and a beautiful rusty color.

FOR THE PIZZA BREAD:

2 teaspoons dry yeast (less than 1 package of yeast)
1 teaspoon sugar
1/3 cup warm water (108 degrees)
1 and 1/4 cups warm water
2 teaspoons honey
2 and 1/2 teaspoons salt
2 tablespoons olive oil
3 and 3/4 cups all-purpose, unbleached flour

THE RUB AND TOPPING:
1 can chipotles en adobo (you will only need a portion)
2 tablespoons fragrant olive oil
1 clove garlic, minced through a press
1 cup of grated Italian Fontina or Monterey Jack

1. Dissolve the yeast and sugar in warm water. Let it proof in a small bowl for about 10 minutes or until puffy. In a large mixing bowl, stir together the yeast mixture, honey, salt, olive oil, and one cup of flour. Beat until well blended. Next add the rest of the flour a little at a time.

2. Turn the dough out onto a floured board and allow it to rest for five to ten minutes while you wash out the bowl and rub it with a few teaspoons of olive oil.

3. Knead the rested dough (it will be easier to handle) for only three minutes. Place dough in the bowl and turn to coat it well with the olive oil. Let it rise about one hour or until doubled.

4. Punch the dough down. You may form your pizza bread or you can refrigerate the dough for several hours, well-protected by plastic wrap so it does not dry out. The refrigerator rest is not necessary but I think it causes a mellowing of the dough, making it easier to handle and you can divide your task into two parts.

5. Oil a baking sheet. If you use a dark, heavy sheet or a baking stone, the result will be a crustier pizza. Punch the dough down again if you placed it in the refrigerator for any period of time. Gently roll it into a freeform shape about 14 inches long and one-inch thick. Use your fingers to push little indentations in the surface of the dough and brush on the mixture of one tablespoon of mashed chipotle en adobo, the olive oil, and the garlic. Reserve the rest of the chipotle in a glass jar. It will keep for

months. Sprinkle with the grated cheese. Allow the pizza bread to rise for only ten minutes and place into a hot 400 degree oven.

6. Bake for 25 to 30 minutes or until bread is golden and crusty.

Eat immediately! It will keep nicely for several hours.

TEXAS JALAPEÑO CORN MUFFINS

These muffins are Texas muffins because they are baked in a tin with huge cups, making only six. The recipe makes 12 normal muffins. These are a little different because the jalapeño chiles and cheese are used as a surprise filling rather than mixed into the rest of the batter. These are a perfect accompaniment to a salad luncheon or a light dinner.

1 cup flour
1 and 1/2 cups yellow cornmeal
1 tablespoon baking powder
1/4 teaspoon baking soda
1/2 teaspoon salt
2 tablespoons sugar
2 eggs
1 cup buttermilk

1/4 cup melted butter
1 cup grated sharp Cheddar, packed in cup
4 jalapeños en escabeche, rinsed, seeded,
  minced
2 tablespoons minced pimiento for color

1. Preheat oven to 400 degrees. Spray Texas muffin cups with baker's spray or rub insides of cups with butter. I prefer the baker's spray because the muffins never stick.

2. Mix the dry ingredients together.

3. Mix the cheese, chiles, and pimiento together. Set aside.

4. Beat the eggs with the buttermilk and stir in the cooled butter. Gently mix the dry and the wet ingredients together. Place about one-third cup of batter in the bottoms of the muffin cups. Place about two tablespoons of the chile mixture on the batter and then place another one-third cup batter on top. Sprinkle a little chile mixture over this batter. The muffins will bake with a chile filling and a decorative top.

5. Bake in the preheated oven for 25 minutes or until golden.

CHAPTER VII

CHOCOLATE TO SOOTHE THE PALATE

Chocolate continues to fascinate me as being as one of the most perfect foods to follow a picante meal with chiles. As has been proven, and I am living testament to this, one can increase endurance by a gradual exposure to capsicums. But after an assault of chile, a soothing chocolate is better than a lick of pure salt, icy beer, dill pickles, ice water, or a loaf of plain French bread. These antidotes are recommended for chile overdose and I have half-heartedly tried them all with various stages of success but I would rather take my cure with chocolate cake. Just this morning, after a breakfast of Huevos Rancheros with New Mexican Red Chile Sauce, we had a cup of cafe con leche (dark coffee with hot milk) and a tiny piece of chocolate cake. The cake, Aunt Jean's French Chocolate Cake, was left over from a dinner given the night before and it tasted supremely better this morning.

The only thing better than chocolate cake for breakfast would be either a cup of thick, custardy chocolate or a chocolate souffle. With chiles preceding it, of course.

AUNT JEAN'S FRENCH CHOCOLATE CAKE

This cake is one of Aunt Jean's greatest accomplishments. She did not make any other dessert because no one would let her. Aunt Jean belonged to my husband, Bob, and he says that she had to bring this cake to every family gathering and every holiday. There is nothing like it. It is so delicate, it tastes like it came from the kitchen of an angel. In her lifetime, Aunt Jean only gave me one gift. This recipe.

THE CAKE:

1/2 cup butter, slightly softened
1 and 1/2 cups sugar
2 whole eggs, beaten
1/2 cup milk, room temperature
1 and 3/4 cup sifted cake flour
1 and 1/2 teaspoons cream of tartar
2 squares bitter chocolate, melted
3/4 cup boiling water
1 teaspoon soda

1. Preheat your oven to exactly 350 degrees. Grease the bottoms of 3 8-inch cake pans and

fit with rounds of parchment paper. Grease the paper with shortening also. Do not grease the sides of the pans, only the bottoms and the tops of the paper. Set aside.

2. After you have measured the one and three-fourths cups of sifted cake flour, sift it three times over a rectangle of wax paper. Then (THIS IS IMPORTANT) sift the cake flour and cream of tartar together SIX TIMES. And make sure that your cream of tartar is fresh. If it is more than two months old, it is not worth the gamble to use. Purchase a fresh can of it for this cake!

3. Cream the butter with your mixer, gradually adding the sugar. Slowly add the beaten eggs and then the milk until all is very well mixed. This will take about two minutes. Next add the sifted flour-cream of tartar mixture, one-half cup at a time. Just stir in until barely blended. Then add the cooled, melted chocolate and mix until completely blended. Get the mixing bowl off the stand and detach the beater. Have a large whisk next to the bowl of cake batter.

4. Have ready on the counter, a glass two-cup measuring cup and the baking soda and

measuring spoons. The teakettle should have two cups of water in it that has been brought to the boil but when I am ready for this crucial step, I turn on the heat so the kettle will again come to the boil in a few seconds. Pour the three-fourths cup boiling water into the measuring cup and quickly add the one teaspoon of baking soda. It will bubble and froth. IMMEDIATELY use the waiting whisk to STIR the foaming water into the cake batter. Stir, but do not beat or whisk, the batter and the water together. Take no more than 15 seconds even if it isn't completely blended. That's okay.

5. Pour the very liquid batter into the waiting cake pans so that they are evenly filled. Immediately place in the preheated oven.

6. Bake for 28 to 30 minutes in the 350 degree oven. A cake tester will come out clean.

7. Allow the cakes to cool on a rack for 10 minutes. Run a knife around the edges and unmold each cake onto a rack to further cool. Do not frost the cakes until an hour or two before you need to serve them. Cover them with plastic wrap after they have cooled.

French Cake Frosting:

3 squares melted semi-sweet chocolate
1 tablespoon very soft butter
1 egg
1/2 cup whipping cream
1 and 1/2 cups powdered sugar
1 teaspoon vanilla extract
1/2 cup chocolate curls or grated chocolate

1. Melt the chocolate and stir in the butter and egg. Beat together until thickened. It should be completely cooled before you add it to the whipped cream or it will immediately deflate the cream.

2. Whip the cream to soft peaks and add the powdered sugar and vanilla.

3. Gradually beat the chocolate mixture into the whipped cream over a bowl of ice. It will take a couple of minutes of beating until it thickens enough to frost the cake but remember this is not a stiff icing.

4. Frost between each layer of cake and then cover the sides lightly and place the remainer of frosting on the top. Use a potato peeler to peel

chocolate curls off a bar of semi-sweet chocolate and, with a spoon, sprinkle the curls over
the top of the cake. Do not use your fingers to
sprinkle or they will melt the chocolate on
contact.

5. Enjoy this lovely cake. If you need to keep
the cake overnight and if the house is over 68
degrees, the cake should be refrigerated.

TRIPLE CHOCOLATE COOKIES

These cookies, with three different kinds of
chocolate, are beautiful to look at and beautiful
to eat. When they are sitting in my glass cookie
jar, they are a giant magnet to anyone entering
the kitchen. I often serve them with coffee after
a meal of enchiladas or mole and they are just
enough.

1 and 1/2 sticks sweet butter (6 oz.)
3 ounces of unsweetened chocolate
1 and 1/2 cups sugar
2 teaspoons vanilla extract
1/2 teaspoon almond extract

2 eggs
2 and 1/4 cups all-purpose flour
1 tablespoon bitter cocoa powder
3/4 teaspoon baking powder
1/2 teaspoon salt
1/2 cups white chocolate pieces or broken
  white chocolate
1 cup bittersweet chocolate chips or chocolate
chunks

1. Melt the butter and unsweetened chocolate together in a saucepan or microwave. Cool for 10 minutes.

2. Beat in the sugar, extracts, and the eggs one at a time.

3. Stir in the dry ingredients. When dough is no longer warm to the touch, stir in the white chocolate pieces and chocolate chips. If the dough is too hot it will simply melt the chips and they will blend into the dough.

4. Drop large tablespoons of cookie batter onto greased baking sheets. Bake in preheated 350 degree oven for 12 minutes. If you bake the cookies too long, they will be dry rather than fudgey. Makes 18-20 large cookies.

MEXICAN WEDDING COOKIES

These cookies are a traditional cookie of Mexico, found at every panaderìa in the small villages or the elegant bakeries of Mexico City. And they always taste different. Here is my version which goes quite well with a platter of Triple Chocolate Cookies.

2 cups all-purpose flour
3/4 cup pecans
1 cup butter, **slightly** *softened*
1/2 cup powdered sugar
1 teaspoon vanilla extract
1/2 teaspoon almond extract
1 cup powdered sugar for rolling cookies

1. Place the pecans in the bowl of a food processor along with one cup of the flour. Using on and off pulsations, grind together until nuts are fine.

2. Beat the sugar with the butter. The butter should not be too soft or the cookie batter will be difficult to work with. Add the extracts.

3. Add the nut-flour mixture to the butter. Beat in the remaining cup of flour. Refrigerate the cookie batter for 20 minutes. Preheat the oven to 350 degrees.

4. Form the batter into balls and place on ungreased baking sheets. Makes about 35 cookies.

5. Bake for 12 minutes.

6. When they have cooled for about 15 minutes. Sprinkle powdered sugar over the tops until they are entirely covered.

NORMA'S BEST IN THE WORLD BROWNIES

Norma does not like rich desserts but she will submit to these brownies or fresh strawberries bathed in Grand Marnier and raspberry sauce. I will submit to both. These particular brownies, to be perfect, must be baked for only the alloted time so they resemble thick fudge with a thin glaze of a crust.

3 squares of unsweetened chocolate
1 cube butter
2 teaspoons vanilla
Pinch of salt
1 and 1/2 cups sugar
2 eggs
1 cup all-purpose flour
1 cup walnuts or pecans, chopped

1. Melt the chocolate and butter together.
Grease and flour an eight by eight pan.

2. Add vanilla and salt to the warm chocolate.
Stir in the sugar until well blended. Beat in one
egg at a time.

3. Next add the flour and the nuts. Stir just
until well blended.

4. BAKE AT EXACTLY 350 DEGREES FOR
25 MINUTES. A toothpick inserted in the
center should have a thin film of chocolate on it
when the brownies are done.

5. Cool for two to three hours (I have refrigerated them when in a hurry) before cutting them
into squares. They will fall apart if you try to
cut them when they are warm.

CHOCOLATE DIPPED TENDER BISCOTTI

My years of seaching for the perfect biscotti ended with these. Biscotti are a dry little cookie meant for dipping into hot coffee or chocolate. I have not yet graduated to dipping them into my wine. Neither should they be so hard as to break your teeth nor so soft as to fall off in your coffee upon dipping.

4 eggs
1 and 1/2 cups sugar
2 teaspoons vanilla
1 teaspoon almond extract
1 tablespoon brandy
4 ounces melted butter
3 and 1/2 cups all-purpose flour
2 teaspoons baking powder
1/4 teaspoon salt
1 cup slivered almonds
12 ounces seme-sweet or bittersweet chocolate
1 and 1/2 tablespoons shortening

1. Preheat oven to 350 degrees. Grease 2 baking sheets or line with baking parchment.

2. Beat eggs and sugar together until well-blended. Add the almond extract, vanilla, brandy, and melted butter. Beat together.

3. Stir all the dry ingredients together and then add to the above liquid ingredients. This will result in a fairly thick dough.

4. Form the dough into three ten-inch long logs. Form two logs on one baking sheet and one log on another sheet. Don't worry if the logs spread out and widen a little. The looser the dough, the more tender the biscotti.

5. Bake for thirty-eight minutes. Cool the logs on the baking sheets for at least one hour. By allowing them to cool down, they will have a finer texture when sliced. Using a serrated knife, cut into one-half inch slices.

6. Place all slices back onto baking sheets. Bake for twelve minutes at 325 degrees and then turn slices so they may toast equally on both sides. Bake another twelve minutes. Change the baking sheets from top to bottom racks at least once during the entire baking time. Watch closely so biscotti do not brown too much. They should color a slight golden. Remove from oven and allow to cool on the baking sheets. They will crisp up more while they cool. Makes about three to three and one-half dozen.

7. Meanwhile melt chocolate and shortening over hot water or in a microwave oven (3 minutes at 90 power). Stir chocolate and shortening and dip each biscotti so half is coated in chocolate. Place on waxed paper until chocolate is set.

INDEX

Chimayo, 40, 69
Chipotle, 16, 114, 131
Cascabel, 115
Dixon, 61, 64
Fresno, 109
Guero, 109
Jalapeño, 109
New Mexican, 39
Mulato, 104
Pasilla (Poblano) 73, 145
Pequin, 116, 123
Serrano, 109
Thai, 113
Chile powder, 24, 133
Chile rajas, 77
Chile sauce, 25
Chiles en nogada, 88
Chile verde, 43
Chili
Fiery chili, 67
Tame chili, 34
Turkey chili, 165
Chipotle
Chile, 16, 14, 131
Chipotle chiles with
  pizza bread, 191
Chipotle cream, 16
Chipotle pork chops, 145
Chipotle sauce with
  meatballs, 160
Honey chipotle barbecue
  sauce, 162
Chipotle corn salsa, 154
Creamy chipotle sauce, 135
Salsa de chipotle, 163
Smoked fire, 164

Chocolate
Aunt Jean's French
  chocolate cake, 199
Chocolate-dipped biscotti, 208
Norma's Best Brownies, 206
Triple chocolate cookies, 203
Cookies
Biscotti, 208
Mexican wedding, 205
Triple chocolate, 203
Corn
Calabacitas, 59
Chipotle corn salsa, 154
Chile pepper salad, 93
Pudding, 22
Creamy soup, 92
Poblano soup, 90
Vegetable stew, 20
Dixon chile, 61, 64
Dried New Mexican, 60
Epazote, 7, 16
Enchiladas
Chicken mole, 104
Santa Fe green, 49
Sonoran, 157
Fresno chiles, 109
Fireman's salsa, 126
Flour tortillas
Traditional, 176
Chips flavored, 182
Green chile sauce, 47
Guero chiles, 109
Guajillo chiles, 116, 128
Jalapeño
Flavored tortilla chips, 182
Rolls, 186
Magic juice, 122

211

RESOURCES

The Chile Shop
109 E. Water Street
Santa Fe, New Mexico 87501
(505)-983-6080
One of the best sources for dried chiles such as Chimayo
and Dixon ground chile.

Chile Pepper Emporium
328 San Felipe Rd.N.W. (Old Town)
Albuquerque, New Mexico 87104
(505)-242-7538
Dried chiles, dried posole, beans, and Care
packages from Southwest.

Green Chile Fix Company
P.O. Box 5463
Santa Fe, New Mexico 87502
Produce the dried green New Mex
chile. Great to use as a spice.

Peppers
4009 N. Brown Ave
Scottsdale, Arizona 85251
(602)990-8347
Arizona source for chiles.

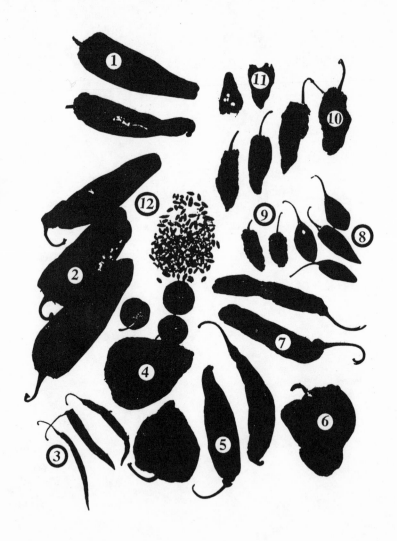

1. NEW MEXICO CHILES
2. CALIFORNIA CHILES
3. JAPONES
4. ANCHOS
5. GUAJILLOS
6. MULATO
7. PASILLA NEGROS

8. JALAPEÑOS (OVEN-DRIED)
9. JALAPEÑOS (SUN-DRIED)
10. CHIPOTLES (MEXICO)
11. CHIPOTLES (U.S.)
12. PEQUINS
13. CASCABELS